The Church of Scotland

A Short History

BY

G. D. HENDERSON, D.D., D.Litt.

PROFESSOR OF CHURCH HISTORY IN
THE UNIVERSITY OF ABERDEEN
AND MASTER OF CHRIST'S COLLEGE

The Church of Scotland Youth Committee

Edinburgh

GLASGOW
Departmental
Libraries
UNIVERSITY

CONTENTS

		PAGE
I.	INTRODUCTORY	1
II.	HOW THE GOSPEL CAME TO SCOTLAND	7
III.	SAINT COLUMBA	14
IV.	THE SCOTLAND OF QUEEN MARGARET	22
V.	THE PRE-REFORMATION CHURCH	31
VI.	THE DAWN OF THE REFORMATION	38
VII.	THE WORK OF JOHN KNOX	46
VIII.	REFORMED SCOTLAND	55
IX.	THE EARLY SEVENTEENTH CENTURY	63
X.	COVENANTERS TRIUMPHANT	70
XI.	THE COVENANTERS UNDER PERSECUTION	77
XII.	CHURCH LIFE IN THE SEVENTEENTH CENTURY	85
XIII.	THE REVOLUTION SETTLEMENT	93
XIV.	THE FIRST SECESSION	101
XV.	THE SECOND SECESSION AND THE MODERATES	109
XVI.	THE EVANGELICAL REVIVAL	117
XVII.	THE VOLUNTARY PRINCIPLE	125
XVIII.	THE DISRUPTION	134
XIX.	SPIRITUAL INDEPENDENCE	143
XX.	THE NATIONAL CHURCH REVIVES	153
XXI.	A CENTURY OF CHANGE	162
XXII.	THE REUNITED CHURCH OF SCOTLAND	170
XXIII.	OUR OWN DAY	178
XXIV.	THE PRESBYTERIAN FAMILY	186
	INDEX	195

"THE CHURCH OF SCOTLAND"

G. D. HENDERSON

CORRIGENDA

The following alterations are added to bring the original text up-to-date in terms of names of organisations, etc.,

Page 4	line 14	*for* "Guildry" *read* "Brigade".
"	line 15	*delete* "or Girls' Association".
Page 97	line 11	*read* "The regiment continued to hold an honoured place in the British Army until it was disbanded" on 14th May, 1968.
Page 165	line 35	*add* "and a further revision in 1972".
Page 169	line 23	*for* "is projected", *read* "was produced in 1959".
Page 171	lines 31 and 32	*delete* "in the attempt at an" *and read* "even broader unions in South India (1947), North India and Pakistan (1970), and many further ecumenical movements".
Page 181	lines 37	*for* "Foreign Mission", *read* "Overseas".
	and 38	*delete* "and on those of the Women's Association".
Page 182	line 12	*delete* "Fishermen and fisher girls".
Pages 191-2		*for* "Empire" and "Dominions" *read* "Commonwealth".
Page 192	line 32	*delete* "Original Secession".
"	line 36	*for* "Continental and Colonial Committee", *read* "Overseas Council".
Page 193	line 10	*After* "Presbyterian Alliances", *add* "(now the World Alliance of Reformed Churches.)"

CHAPTER I.

INTRODUCTORY.

The Challenge of a New Day.—We of to-day live very definitely in a new world. We are aware of conditions and circumstances—domestic, educational, international—that have something unique about them. It is plain that, however much romance attaches to the ships of the Elizabethan navy that swept the Spanish main, they would be utterly useless for the times to which we look forward. We feel that likewise many of the ways and ideas of other days will not do for us. We must think out the whole business afresh. There is thus a temptation to turn scornfully from history, and to follow Nietzsche in despising our ancestral generations and concentrating devotion upon generations still to come. We are apt to think of the past as an 'old fogey,' a warning and a failure.

It is true that we ought to be up to date. The Church *must* be up to date. If there is to be attainment, equipment and methods require to be the very latest. The future that lies before us will need special handling. Most centuries and generations to some extent have been faced with a corresponding task, and indeed the Church has, in fact, age after age, slowly but surely succeeded in adapting itself to new situations. One thinks of the way in which it righted itself after Galileo, and after Darwin. The process of adaptation must go on. Certainly the Church requires clearly to keep before it the aim of effectively bringing Christ to the world of Now. No pains should be spared to this end. We must, as Shakespere says, " be stirring with the morrow."

Or, quoting Tennyson, we may say—

> "Call me not so often back,
> Silent voices of the dead,
> Toward the lowland ways behind me,
> And the sunlight that is gone!
> Call me rather, silent voices,
> Forward to the starry track
> Glimmering up the heights beyond me,
> On, and always on!"

Eternal Factors.—It must at the same time be realised that human nature does not change much with the progress of the ages. All the latest inventions leave men fundamentally still the same. We see how far this is the case if we turn to poetry and note that all the poets in all the centuries have continued to treat of exactly the same few subjects. Language changes. Dress changes. Means of transport change. Methods of government change. But the human soul with its deepest needs is just as it was in far-off Egypt or Israel. Men's minds and hearts work much as they have always done. The same motives turn up everywhere. The same types of crisis occur. The study of history is useful if it even does no more than convince us of this and give us a sense of proportion. We can be satisfied that the important problems of the future will not differ essentially from those of other days. The experience of the past has something to teach us about those things that really matter. History deals with eternal factors.

Our Inheritance.—To some extent each generation has to learn for itself. It is often remarked how little one age seems to profit by the advice of its predecessor. We have to learn to walk and to talk. At the same time we do not have to invent limbs and tongue. However original and revolutionary we feel, we cannot shake free from the past. Our future begins from our present, and the present is to a large extent made up of the past. The path for good or ill is laid down for us. The marvellously contrived bodies that we have tell a very old story. Our race, century, blood-group, family, sex, opportunities, quality of brain, and much else are given and go to constitute the instrument through which we shall always have to work. The powers with which the new situation in our future will have to be met will be exactly the same as those with which people long ago met their new situations; the same faith and courage, the same unselfishness and charity, the same spirit of self-consecration. And the temptations will not be different: "There hath no temptation taken you but such as is common to men." There is good reason for examining and consulting the past.

When, as Christians, we look back upon the centuries, we recall first of all the debt we owe to the Grace of God in Christ our Saviour. What kind of a world would it be to-day had that revelation of the sovereignty and love of God never been vouchsafed? The Christian is born with a silver spoon in his mouth. He has spiritual standards provided and available. He has the Bible, with what it has preserved and made definite. There is the history gathered up in the Bible, and reaching back to the far distant past, to Babylon where thousands of years ago men decided that there should be seven days in our week and sixty minutes in our hour. There is the Jewish, Greek, and Roman contribution. There are the Creeds, the body of doctrine which everywhere, always and by all, was accepted within the Church; the inheritance of liturgical and devotional practice and aids behind our present Sunday services; the institutional guidance of the centuries as to Church government and discipline, which has made us, in particular, Presbyterians. There are great periods with such special messages as Monasticism or Gothic architecture; there are splendid traditions, such as those laid down by Thomas Aquinas or Calvin; there have been serious spiritual crises, such as the Reformation or the less tremendous, but for us determining crises, of Scottish history; there have been dominating and inspiring personalities—Augustine, Bernard, Columba, Luther, John Wesley. It is a marvellous store, not merely of information, but of encouragement and consolation and power.

The Church to which we belong.—As members of the Church of Scotland we should attempt to understand our present in the light of our past with a view to our future. Perhaps we belong to a Bible Class. It is connected with some Christian congregation and conducted by the minister or his assistant or a deaconess. It meets in a hall of the church. We sing one or two hymns. There is a prayer. We are given a lesson about something in the Bible, or about mission work abroad or social problems at home. We were baptised when we were infants, and our parents then made promises that they would bring us up in the love and service of Jesus Christ, whom they professed to accept as their Saviour. By and by we shall become communicants, and shall sit down with crowds of others and receive the bread and the wine. We shall be expected to attend regularly in church on Sundays, worshipping God in praise and prayer and hearing the preaching of God's Word, and being encouraged by the fellowship of other members to live as Jesus would like us to live. The minister wears gown and bands. There is an organ and a choir to lead the singing. We are expected to take a share in the activities of the congregation, to teach children in Sunday School, to help with Girls' Guildry or Boys' Brigade or Girls' Association, or some other week-day organisation, and to assist in providing or collecting money for religious purposes. The leading men in the congregation are elders and deacons, and we hear of session meetings to deal with congregational business.

There are other congregations where we know that much the same kind of movement goes on. We read in 'Life and Work' of the schemes of the Church of Scotland, which aim at spreading Christian influence at home and abroad. Our minister tells us that he has to attend a Presbytery meeting. We know that he has been visiting the homes of people who belong to the Church and of others whom he is trying to interest in Church life, and that he has been conducting services in connection with funerals and marriages. The ladies of the congregation have been working hard to arrange a sale of work under the Woman's Guild to raise money for the work of the congregation and of the Church of Scotland. Perhaps the Moderator of the General Assembly comes to take a special service some Sunday. Some of our friends go to Churches that are different from ours in beliefs and practices—Christian churches, not Church of Scotland and Presbyterian, but possibly Episcopalian or Baptist or Roman Catholic. A missionary will tell us of people in other countries who are not Christian at all, or we may have a visit from a Presbyterian minister from England or America. And again there are people living near us who do not seem ever to go to church.

Why are these things so ? How does it come about that we have churches and ministers and Bible Classes ? It is a matter of history. To see what it all means we have to go back into the past and watch it growing up through the centuries. We cannot appreciate any institution properly unless we know how it has come to be. The widespread and deeply rooted organisation to which we belong, with its doctrine, worship, government, and discipline, is the result of a long and interesting and eventful process of development —the History of the Church of Scotland.

Inspiration from the Past.—There is inspiration in the study of this past. Let us by way of illustration imagine a minister in some remote parish, with his monotonous routine, his comparatively petty daily occupations and interruptions, the worries of a handful of not very exciting or exemplary parishioners. He will not be without friends, and God is always a present help. But he may slip into a rut, may feel that he is not making anything of it, that instead of producing a spiritual transformation, he has scarcely succeeded in keeping people even as Christian as they were. He may lose heart, become soured, wonder if it is worth while, may even cease to try. Think of him, however, going to the annual General Assembly of the Church of Scotland in Edinburgh in the month of May. Nothing very remarkable may happen. No momentous decisions may be made. No unforgettable speeches may be heard. But he finds himself in a great crowd of people all intensely interested. He comes to have a 'feel' of the Church as a whole, as a vast organism with life throbbing in all its distant limbs and parts. He realises that he belongs to something that undoubtedly is worth while ; and his own part becomes important because it is a part, a necessary part, of a great whole.

A similar effect upon a larger scale may result for all of us from a study of history. One discovers that one's own congreation in a small corner belongs to a mighty institution with wonderful traditions, a church which can be traced back through the centuries, past the Disruption and the Secessions to the Covenanters and to John Knox, and away back still to Columba and Ninian, and back further yet to the first disciples gathered with their Lord and Master round the first Supper Table. Each member of the Church of Scotland is in that succession. We fill up the gaps left where others have stood down. All that is behind us is ours. The same God who worked then works now. He uses us as He used St Peter and St Andrew, Knox and Melville, Alexander Henderson and Ebenezer Erskine, William Robertson, Thomas Chalmers and Norman Macleod. All these, great leaders as history shows them to have been, were like ourselves, unable to do anything but by the Grace of God; just like ourselves, earthen vessels. It is human beings through whom God achieves His purposes. Nor is it only leaders whom He requires to bring in His Kingdom. There is no one who is not under call to serve; no one whom God does not expect to be in some degree a maker of history. The past will rouse us to a sense of our privileges and our responsibilities.

At the moment we are thinking chiefly of religious developments; but all history is one. Besides causes which are religious there are others, especially economic and political, and these are all the time active and inter-related. We must not forget them even when we abstract and fix our minds specially upon the religious aspect of the history of our land.

Nor must we lose sight of the fact that we make another abstraction when we concentrate our attention on the history of one nation. However important and however much beloved, ours is but an extremely small country. We must remember the background of European and world history. Above all we must try to realise that our Church of Scotland is not an institution which exists merely for its own sake, or even for Scotland's sake. Our national Church has a part to play in the drama of human development in accordance with God's will. God is sovereign and God is love. He is the creator of the ends of the earth, God and Father of all. We have to try to see our Scottish church life in this setting, see it in the light of eternity, and so to bring it more and more to minister to His Glory.

Books to read :—

E. Bevan, 'Christianity.' (Home University Library.)
R. L. Mackie, 'Short History of Scotland.' (1931.)

CHAPTER II.

HOW THE GOSPEL CAME TO SCOTLAND.

THERE is a legend that the Three Wise Men of the Christmas story were very different in years, and that to the oldest Jesus appeared to be already aged, to the next, who was in middle life, he showed himself as a middle-aged man, while to the third, a mere youth, the Saviour seemed still young. The story is meant to remind us that Jesus is the Light of the World (John viii. 12), the Desire of all Nations (Haggai ii. 7). His Word is for all. He is the particular saviour each one requires. We speak of Christianity as a 'universal' religion, and universal (meant for all) is the proper significance of the word 'catholic,' when used of the Church. The Gospel of Christ is "the power of God unto Salvation to everyone that believeth" (Rom. i. 16).

Christianity.—On the notice hung upon the cross of Calvary, the kingship of Jesus was proclaimed in Greek and Latin and Hebrew. These languages under God represented the three great civilisations of those days, which so wonderfully combined to spread the "good tidings of great joy which shall be to all people" (Luke ii. 10). Jesus was born of Hebrew race, and made use of the religious customs of the Jews, their Old Testament, their belief in One God, their high moral tone. Jews were widely scattered throughout the world, and their synagogues everywhere offered a starting-point to early Christian missionaries, such as St Paul. Many Gentiles, or non-Jews, who "feared God" (Acts x. 2) used to interest themselves in the synagogue services, and through these the Gospel reached others outside Judaism.

Greek, the language in which the New Testament was written, the language of Antioch where the followers of Jesus were first called Christians (Acts xi. 26), was known over the wide territories which had been conquered by Alexander the Great (died 330 B.C.), and this made the work of the first missionaries easier, since they had no foreign tongue to learn. Further, the idea of " one God and Father of all " (Eph. iv. 6) was not too difficult for people accustomed to a world ruled by one man, as it had been in the days of Alexander. Greek thought as it had come down from famous ancient philosophers such as Plato (died 347 B.C.) and Aristotle (died 322 B.C.) helped to form the system of Christian doctrine and belief as we find it in the Creeds.

At the time of Christ, the known world, including Palestine, was mostly under the government of the Romans, who spoke Latin. The cause of Christ was assisted by the peace and order and unity which Roman rule provided, and also by the splendid roads which the Romans made through every country, and by which missionaries and merchants might travel in safety. Roman justice, too, was very fair and gave freedom to preach the new faith anywhere.

In view of all this, it is not surprising that the Gospel spread rapidly. To Mesopotamia and Parthia in the East, to Egypt and the North of Africa, to Asia Minor, to Greece and Italy, the message was carried. Soon there were Christians as far off as Spain and the South of France, and presently comes the first rumour that the Word has been heard in Britain.

Tertullian, writing in North Africa about 200 A.D., refers to " haunts of the Britons, inaccessible to the Romans, but subjugated to Christ." Origen, about forty years later, in more than one of his sermons preached in Palestine, speaks of Christians in Britain. Bede, the first great English Church historian (died 735 A.D.), says that in the persecution under the Emperor Diocletian, many persons in Britain died as martyrs for the Faith, and he describes particularly the martyrdom of St Alban in 305 A.D. It is quite certain that at a Church Council which met at Arles in the South of France in 314 A.D. three bishops from Britain were present, and after that date we are left in no doubt as to the steady growth of the British Church. We do not know by whom Christianity was first brought to Britain. Neither, indeed, is it known who first preached the Gospel at Rome or in Egypt. Christianity was spread, not merely by great missionary Apostles, but also by the example and effort of simple Christians. Monnica, the mother of St. Augustine, was led to Christ by a slave nurse-maid. A barbarian tribe in the Caucasus was converted to Christianity by a woman whom they had taken captive in war. Wrecked merchants gave Christianity to Abyssinia. The anti-Christian Celsus complained that Christianity was even being privately spread by "workers in wool and leather and fullers and persons of the most uninstructed and rustic character."

The Church in the Roman Empire.—By 313 A.D. Christianity had become strong amongst all classes throughout the Roman Empire, and the Emperor Constantine decided for the liberty of the Christians, making it legal to be a Christian, declaring himself a follower of Christ and being eventually baptised. With the exception of Julian (361-363 A.D.) all the succeeding emperors were professing Christians, and finally in 392 A.D. the Emperor Theodosius made Christianity the official religion of the Roman Empire.

From the days of Constantine it was no longer dangerous to profess oneself a disciple of Christ, and people crowded into the Church, so that by the close of the century a profession of the Christian religion was quite normal and usual throughout the civilised world. Christianity had, in fact, conquered the Roman Empire. From very small and simple beginnings, the Church had become powerful and flourishing, and had not only royal support but leaders of genius. The resources of the Church rapidly increased, and it had magnificent buildings at the greater centres. A century of earnest study and keen discussion had clarified the Christian theology. The worship of the Church had also matured, and very dignified liturgies or forms of service were in use. There were celebrated preachers such as Chrysostom, the 'golden mouthed.' Bishops, presbyters and deacons, with certain minor orders, had become the recognised ministry, and alongside of the ordinary clergy there had appeared also monks, such as St Anthony, who gave up the world to devote themselves entirely to the salvation of their souls.

One Western leader of Monasticism must be specially noted because of his dominating influence within the Celtic Church. St Martin (died about 397 A.D.), whose name is remembered at Martinmas (11th November), a soldier and the son of a soldier, pictures of whom generally show him in the act of giving away half of his military cloak to a shivering beggar, became famous for patience and humility " beyond all human standards," adopted a religious life of extreme rigour and self-denial, was made Bishop of Tours in France, and there founded a large monastery which developed into the chief training school of missionaries for the Celtic area. He was a man of commanding personality, most winning manner, complete consecration to Christ's service, and intense concern for souls.

Scotland and St Ninian.—The Roman Empire at no period included Scotland. Agricola led his legions into the country in 80 B.C., and later there were occasional raids north of the Forth. A wall between the Forth and the Clyde was built and afterwards strengthened, and the part of the country south of this remained to some extent a sphere of Roman influence, but the border-line of the Empire was rather the strongly fortified wall of Hadrian, which joined the Solway and the Tyne in the North of England. The Romans occupied England for centuries—longer than the British have been in India—and they greatly affected the whole life of the people. Roman influence to a small extent crossed the borders of Empire. It was thus that Christianity reached Persia and Armenia and the Goths, and in this way also Scotland first heard of Christ.

The country was not without civilisation, and art was wonderfully advanced, but as compared with the centre of Empire the people were barbarous and the land was undeveloped, with much tangled forest and treacherous bog. The inhabitants of the greater part of what we now call Scotland were Picts, but in the south we find Britons with a stronghold at Dumbarton, and in the west Scots were beginning to come in from Northern Ireland. In later times Angles invaded the south-east, Danes attacked the north-east, and Norwegians took possession of the Western Islands. For centuries to come there was nothing that could be called a nation.

The religion of the people was crude, superstitious, and uninspiring, and gave way easily before the clear superiority of the Christian faith. We must not forget that Scotland was a heathen country won for Christ by foreign missionary enterprise.

The first name in the story of the Scottish Church is that of St Ninian. We hear of him from Bede and from the later and less reliable, but not entirely valueless, work of Ailred. He must have been born about the middle of the fourth century, and was apparently the son of a chief in the Solway district who had become a Christian under Roman influence. Ninian was "accurately instructed at Rome" in Christian truth. Britons, we know, did at this period take advantage of the opportunities of travel which the Empire provided. Jerome, writing in 386 from Bethlehem about the numerous pilgrims, says: "The Briton, sundered from our world, no sooner makes progress in religion, than he leaves the setting sun in quest of a spot of which he knows only through Scripture and common report."

And it was natural to go to Rome. Ammianus Marcellinus writing at this time says: "In every quarter of the world Rome is still looked up to as the mistress and queen of the earth, and the name of the Roman people is respected and venerated." While in Italy, Ninian might well come across some of the most celebrated figures in Church History. From 381 to 385 A.D. St Jerome, one of the most brilliant students of the Bible, was at Rome, and everyone knew him and was talking about him. St Ambrose was Bishop at Milan from 374 to 397. He ranks amongst the most distinguished of Christian leaders, preachers, and writers. The baptism of St Augustine in 387 created a sensation in the Church. He had been in Italy for some time and remained there for a year or so longer before returning to North Africa where his outstanding work as a theologian was done, and where he wrote his 'Confessions.'

But it would seem that the main influence with Ninian was that of St Martin of Tours, with whom he must have lived and worked for some time in France. It was from Martin that Ninian learned how to set about his life-work. When he returned to his native district, Ninian was fully trained and in every way qualified for his task. Bede calls him "a most revered bishop, and a most holy man."

He settled at Whithorn in a peaceful district in the very South of Scotland close to the Solway. There are interesting remains in the neighbourhood to-day, St Ninian's Cave and some monumental stones of an early period, as well as ruins of later buildings which help us to remember what a famous centre of mission work the place once was. Ninian built a church and monastery to which the name Candida Casa (White House) was given, apparently in imitation of St Martin's great establishment at Tours. Bede says the church was of stone, "a custom unfamiliar to the Britons." This must have been about 400 A.D., soon after the death of St Martin. St Ninian's work continued steadily for some thirty years, for he is supposed to have lived till 432 A.D.

Beginnings of the Church in Scotland.—Disciples came to St Ninian's monastery from various districts, and eventually became leaders of Christian enterprise, evangelising the pagan population and ministering to them. The life of the monks was simple and hard. St Martin believed in asceticism—that is, a way of life which treats the body as an enemy of the soul, disdaining comfort and company. The Celtic Church was clearly very much in earnest. How far St Ninian's influence extended is not known, and the problem has given rise to differences of opinion amongst those interested. It is, however, certain that students from Northern Ireland came to Candida Casa, and on their return did much to form the character of the Church in that part of the world. There was, for example, Finnian, who became head of the important monastery at Moville (near Belfast) where St Columba received part of his training. It is also certain that men from Candida Casa worked across the Solway south of Hadrian's Wall in what we now call England. St Martin's Church at Brampton is one part of the evidence. The parts of Scotland within easy reach of Whithorn would naturally have a first call upon the missionary interest of St Ninian and his followers. There are traces of his work in Ayrshire and in Bute. Tradition records that it was Ninian who consecrated the first burial-ground at Glasgow.

Beyond the Forth and Clyde wall the Romans had pushed their way to Aberdeenshire, as roads and camp sites still bear witness; and pedlars with their goods and missionaries with their Gospel would naturally follow this old line of march if they wished to go north. We consequently find St Ninian's Church close to Stirling, and his name also survives at Blairgowrie (Perthshire), Arbirlot (Angus), Dunnottar (Kincardine), Methlick (Aberdeenshire), and elsewhere near the same route. More remarkable is it to have the name of Ninian associated with old religious sites in Glenurquhart (Inverness-shire), Navidale (Sutherland), and even as far north as Dunrossness (Shetland). There is nothing to show that St Ninian himself had visited those places, but the thirty years during which he was head of Candida Casa and the period immediately after his death may well have produced some such chain of stations.

Perhaps it would not be possible for Candida Casa to keep much hold upon places that lay so far afield, and we may suppose that in some districts little permanent impression would be left. We hear of "apostate Picts" soon after St Ninian's time—Picts who had once accepted Christ but had later fallen back into their old ways. Nevertheless, a beginning had been made, and it was the result of one man's self-dedication. St Ninian heard the call to missionary service and undertook, not just an individual adventure, but a systematic campaign, training a succession of zealous young Christians to show forth Christ and offer His salvation and establish His rule. The work of a missionary is apt to be hard, lonely, dangerous, disappointing. It needs faith and courage, and, still more, charity, but above all a sense of communion with Him who gave Himself for man. We look back with admiration and gratitude to those who were the first to tell the Gospel story in Scotland.

Books to read :—

J. A. Duke, 'History of the Church of Scotland to the Reformation.' (1937.)

W. D. Simpson, 'St Ninian and the Origins of the Christian Church in Scotland.' (1940.)

CHAPTER III.

SAINT COLUMBA.

Christianity in Ireland.—From Britain the Christian message crossed to Ireland. St Patrick (389-461 A.D.) was of British origin, and it is sometimes claimed that he was born at Kilpatrick on the Clyde. When after many adventures he began his great work as the Apostle of Ireland (432 A.D.) there were already Christians in that country. We know of them from his writings, and also from a Latin writer (Prosper of Aquitaine) who under the date 431 refers to "the Scots believing in Christ." The Scots at that time had their home in Ireland and only appeared in Britain as raiders. Christianity spread rapidly among them and among the other peoples of the island, Candida Casa being for a time one of the chief influences.

Another famous name in the early Irish Church is that of St Bride (450-523 A.D.), of whom many beautiful tales are told and whom an old Argyllshire song describes as "the milkmaid of the smooth white palms, Brigit of the clustering hair, golden brown." And the third name that is celebrated for missionary endeavour in those far-off days in Ireland is that of St Columba. A contemporary chronicler (Marianus Scotus) speaks of "Ireland, the island of saints, to a sublime degree, full of holy men and innumerable wonders"; but none have left more sacred memories than St Patrick, St Bride, and St Columba.

Irish monasteries were (like that of St Martin of Tours) intensely missionary. One medieval chronicler (Walahfrid) says that with the Scots the habit of travelling became well-nigh second nature. St Columbanus (540-615 A.D.) did marvellous work in Burgundy, Switzerland, and Northern

Italy, and his disciple, St Gall (550-627 A.D.), and other Irishmen also served on the Continent. There was plenty for them to do, for by their time a great change had taken place on the face of Europe. From about 400 A.D. swarms of pagan or heretic barbarians had been overflowing the borders of the Roman Empire, everywhere destroying on their march the evidences of its civilisation and of its Christianity. Some of them poured from German territory through France into Italy. Roman troops had to be withdrawn from Britain to engage in the war of defence, but Rome was captured and plundered and almost destroyed in 410. Soon the barbarians were also invading the South and East of England, wiping out the traces of Roman rule, and leaving the British Church alive only in the remoter districts of the West. Thus by and by there were whole new nations to be Christianised.

Irish missionaries also came to Scotland. St Brendan of Clonfert did mission work in some of the Western Islands off the Scottish coast before the middle of the sixth century. A number of the adventurers were from the monastery of Bangor, south of Belfast; as, for example, St Moluag (died 592 A.D.), who made Lismore (Argyllshire) the headquarters of his missionary campaigns. There were also native evangelists at work in this period. We may mention St Kentigern (St Mungo), who lived at the same time as St Columba. His name is closely associated with Glasgow, and with revival of the Faith in Strathclyde. The names of many saints survive in local traditions, but of the men themselves little is known, and sometimes the names are hopelessly corrupt. In most cases we cannot tell even the century in which they laboured, or whether the name applies to one man or to several.

There can, however, be no doubt that work for Christ was going on in what we call Scotland before Columba and independent of him, while St Donnan (died 618), St Maelrubha (died 722), and others who have left traces of later extensive missionary enterprise seem likewise to have been independent workers.

St Columba's Early Life—Irish influence in Scotland is best known from the story of St Columba. His reputation owes something to the fact that he was so fortunate as to have an unusually able biographer. 'The Life of St Columba' by St Adamnan (ninth Abbot of Iona, died 704 A.D.) may seem at first glance a mere conglomeration of impossible stories such as compose so many lives of Saints. But read with intelligence it yields what may be accepted as a very reliable portrait of St Columba and an excellent guide to the religious and social conditions of the period.

St Columba was born in Northern Ireland in 521 A.D. His parents were Christians and both belonged to prominent families, so that he grew up naturally to a position of influence in the Church. His education for the ministry he owed largely to British Christianity, for he was for a time under Finnian of Moville (of the school of Candida Casa), and was also under Finnian of Clonard (who had been trained in Wales).

In due course Columba became a priest. He made himself famous as a founder of monasteries. In 546 he started one which was the beginning of the present town of Londonderry, and he was later responsible for establishments at Durrow and Kells, which became celebrated centres of learning. In this manner he lived and worked in Ireland till he was over forty years of age. Then came a crisis with regard to which different stories are told.

One tale is that Columba made a copy of a version of the Psalms in the beautiful script of the time, but secretly, without the permission of the owner of the version, who, when the matter came to light, demanded possession of the copy and had his claim allowed by the High King of Tara in the characteristically Irish judgment: "To every cow her calf, to every book its copy." Columba appealed to his clan, and a sanguinary battle at Culdrevny resulted, for his connection with which he was presently excommunicated by a Church Synod, and accepted as his penance exile from Ireland and the winning of as many souls as there had been lives lost in the feud.

The battle is otherwise explained as due to Columba's indignation at the action of the High King in allowing a man to be put to death who had placed himself under the saint's protection.

Adamnan says merely that "in the second year after the battle of Culedrebine . . . wishing to make a pilgrimage for Christ from Ireland to Britain, he sailed forth"; and later he refers to St Columba's "excommunication by a certain Synod for some venial and quite excusable causes," and indicates that the excommunication was removed.

St Columba strikes one as a type quite likely to become involved in dispute, and more suited to the position of a leader than to that of a subordinate or a colleague. In the succeeding period he paid occasional visits to Ireland. And when he settled in Iona he was still amongst people of his own race, and the conditions of life were very similar to those to which he had been accustomed.

The Scots from Ireland had begun drifting into what is now Argyll in the fifth century, and about the beginning of the sixth the territory which they had appropriated became the more or less independent kingdom of Dalriada. Christianity was generally if perhaps somewhat vaguely accepted. The only other organised authority in Scotland was the Pictish kingdom, whose capital lay on the River Ness.

St Columba in Scotland.—It was in 563 A.D. that St Columba settled on the small island of Iona, just out of sight of his native land. In this strategic position he and his fellow-monks constructed a rude monastic establishment. Of this no trace now remains. The cathedral and the ruins which one can visit to-day belong to later periods. There was a little chapel to which the monks were summoned by hand-bell for worship at different hours throughout each day according to monastic usage. There was the abbot's hut where St Columba lived in true ascetic simplicity. The room in which with pen and ink-horn and parchment he transcribed the Scriptures, where he studied such manuscripts as the little monastery might come to possess, and where he interviewed those who wished to consult him, had a wooden floor; but he slept on the bare earth with a stone for a pillow, and he was unwearied in fasting and watching. Adamnan says: "He could not pass the space even of a single hour without applying himself either to prayer, or reading, or writing, or to some manual labour."

The monks had separate cells, but all fed together in the refectory, and there was accommodation for guests, who are frequently mentioned by Adamnan. Round this collection of buildings was a roughly constructed wall, chiefly of earth and rubble, and outside would be mill, kiln, storehouses, byre and stable, and the "little fields" with the necessary crops. The monks had to provide themselves with food by ploughing, sowing, reaping, ingathering, threshing, winnowing, grinding. We hear of the slaughter of cattle and sheep; seals procured for food; milking; the baking of bread; salt evidently rather scarce; wine; fishing; and even venison and roast pig. There was occupation with the repair of buildings, the collection of rushes for the floors, and, for a special few, the copying of manuscripts. The costume of the monks included a long woollen undergarment, a cowl, sandals, and, on occasion, a white tunic.

From time to time Columba, staff in hand and with one or two companions, made journeys to the mainland and into the territory of the Picts where he had to speak through an interpreter. Some of the work which he undertook was that of a preacher of the Gospel, baptising infants or converts, hearing the confession of the sinful and imposing penance, advising people in trouble, even healing the sick. Some of his missions were political. Thus he had a memorable interview with Brude, the ruler of the Picts, and he had much to do with the election of Aidan to be king of Dalriada. Travelling was not always easy. We hear of robbers, of a village burnt down, of storms, of the hostility of Druid priests, of a murderous assault with a spear, of danger from a wild boar, of a struggle with a monster in the River Ness.

Columba laboured in Scotland for over thirty years, and died on 6th June 597 in the very year in which Pope Gregory sent St Augustine of Canterbury to resume the Christianising of Southern England. Adamnan's account of the last days of St Columba is a justly famous piece of literature, and tells how the saint, weary with age, went on a cart to visit the brethren at their work, and blessed the island and the islanders. On the Lord's Day at Mass, "suddenly with eyes raised heavenwards, the countenance of the venerable man is seen to be suffused with a ruddy glow, for, as it is written, 'when the heart is glad, the countenance blossoms,' for in that hour he also saw an angel of the Lord hovering above." He went to visit the granary, and on coming out sat down to rest, and the white horse that carried the milk-pails came up and laid its head on his breast. He climbed the little hill that overlooked the monastery, and stood gazing at it, and then with uplifted hands commended it to the blessing of God. Returning to his hut, he sat down to transcribe Psalm 34, but only reached verse 10: "They that seek the Lord shall not want any good thing." He went to the little church in the evening and afterwards in bed addressed his last words of advice to the brethren, and finally when the bell tolled at midnight he hurried to the church and was found dying before the altar.

St Columba was a man of very marked and distinguished personality, a man of deep piety with a lifetime's devotion to religious practice, a tireless worker in the service of Christ, a man of education, not without poetic skill, possessed of a voice at once sweet and powerful, able to rule, but also to win the love of those about him, compassionate to penitents, fond of animals, endowed with common-sense. He was not above the superstitions of his age, and he suffered from defects of temper, being masterful and even vindictive, as quick to curse as to bless, but he stood out above all others in his day in Scotland as a leader, and his missionary statesmanship did much to bring together the Picts and Scots under a common faith and so to create the Scottish nation.

St Columba established Christianity in Scotland. Since his work was done there has been no turning back, and so he may well be called the Apostle of Scotland. None has left a deeper impression upon our country's soul.

The Celtic Church.—It has to be noted that the Church represented by St Columba had for about a hundred and fifty years been living in isolation. The tide of barbarian invasion had washed across the Continent in such a way as almost completely to cut off the Christians in Britain and Ireland from Rome. In that long period changes had naturally taken place in outlook and practice, and it is therefore not surprising to find St Columba's followers doing a number of things in a different way from that to which the Church elsewhere had become accustomed.

Pope Gregory the Great (died 604 A.D.), whose interest had been attracted to England by the sight of some fair-complexioned English boys for sale in the slave market at Rome, sent St Augustine to convert these pagans who had settled in Britain. The missionaries found that Christianity had actually survived in the West of England from the time when the Romans had ruled the land, and presently those differences of customs were discovered, and it was only slowly that the Britons were persuaded to fall into line. By and by St Augustine's followers came into touch with the Celtic Church in the North.

Some time after the death of St Columba, Iona had by royal request sent St Aidan to what is now the South-East of Scotland and the North-East of England, and the pagan settlers there had been won for Christianity. A great monastery arose at Whitby under St Hilda in 657 A.D. and another at Old Melrose where St Cuthbert became a monk in 651 A.D. Christianity spread rapidly southwards, and at last the missionaries from Iona and those from Canterbury met. Once more the problem of the difference in practice arose. A conference took place at Whitby in 664 A.D., Iona being represented by St Colman and Canterbury by St Wilfrid; and the local ruler, who presided, gave the decision in favour of the latter, because, while the Celtic tradition claimed St Columba as its main authority, the other boasted the support of St Peter. "He is the door-keeper," said the king, "whom I will not contradict . . . lest when I come to the gates of the kingdom of heaven there should be none to open them, he being my adversary who is proved to have the keys." Serious disputes sometimes arise from what seem trifling causes. In this case the differences were not great, but feeling was strong.

The Celtic Church observed Easter according to an old method of calculating dates that recent science had shown to be mistaken; it is always difficult to persuade people that what has long been accepted may not after all be correct. All priests had a small part of the head shaved, but fashions in the matter of the tonsure had changed in the course of time, and the Celtic Church was found continuing an old way, and was by no means eager to give it up. In most parts of Christendom religious ordinances were provided by priests, monks not being concerned in this work, but merely in the care of their own souls; whereas in Celtic lands the priests were all monks with a communal life. Bishops in the Church for the most part had territorial districts or dioceses over which they ruled, but in Celtic lands divisions were tribal, and the chief Church authority was the abbot of the monastery which supplied ecclesiastical ordinances, there being among the monks bishops who were held in particular honour and who were responsible for the ordination of clergy. St Columba himself belonged, not to the higher order of bishops, but to the lower order of presbyters, and yet he had bishops subordinate to him in jurisdiction. Iona seems for a time to have had a special position over such other missionary stations as were founded by St Columba or his followers.

At the time of the conference at Whitby it was only the work of Iona in Northumbria that was affected, but in 686 A.D. St Adamnan of Iona was won over to the practices recommended by those who were in direct touch with the Church on the Continent, and in 717 Nechtan, king of the Picts, followed his example. After that it was simply a matter of time before the whole Church in Scotland was in line with general custom elsewhere.

Books to read :—

J. A. Duke, 'The Columban Church.' (1932.)
Adamnan, 'Life of St Columba.' (Huyshe's edition.)
W. Douglas Simpson, 'The Historical St Columba.' (1927.)

CHAPTER IV.

THE SCOTLAND OF QUEEN MARGARET.

Development of Church and Nation.—We have considered how Christianity first reached Scotland, and have watched it gradually establishing itself as the religion of the people. There follows a long period about which we know very little. The various races and many tribes whose homes were within the area now named Scotland had still nothing of common spirit or national feeling. Life was at the level of 'existence' rather than at that of 'wellbeing.' Seeking food, keeping some kind of dwelling in repair, protecting themselves and their families from wild animals, indulging in warfare against a neighbouring tribe were the important interests of one generation after another in a country that was largely untamed and uncultivated and sparsely populated, and where anything like a town was yet unknown.

Fighting went on intermittently between Picts and Scots, until at length the two peoples were united about 843 A.D. under King Kenneth Macalpin. But before that the daring Vikings from Norway had discovered that the Hebrides and the West Coast of Scotland were worth raiding. Iona suffered terribly at their hands on several occasions, the last being in 825 when the Abbot Blathmac and his monks were massacred at the altar on refusing to betray the hiding place of the precious shrine that contained the remains of St Columba. The district around Candida Casa seems also to have been pillaged, and to have been for some time without religious ordinances. More than one Scottish king died fighting against the Norsemen. Norwegian rule in the Hebrides continued till 1266, and the Orkneys and Shetlands only became part of the Scottish kingdom in 1472. The Danes were also involved in the raiding of the Scottish coast, particularly in the East where local tradition still points out the sites of fierce battles with these invaders. Relations with English and Danish rulers in the South were likewise frequently a matter of concern, and territorial border-lines varied from time to time. Slowly peace and unity emerged from this chaos.

When we reach a more reliably recorded period we find that the Church has not only survived this time of trial, but has strengthened its hold upon the people and become better organised. The Scots Kirk (*Ecclesia Scoticana*) is first mentioned as such in 878 A.D. Dunkeld had for a time succeeded Iona as the Christian headquarters, but by 906 the leadership of the Church had passed to the bishop whose seat was at St Andrews. This was an old religious foundation, specially revered because of the legend that bones of the Apostle were buried there, a story which by the tenth century had led to the acceptance of St Andrew as the patron saint of the kingdom and of the St Andrew's Cross as the national emblem.

But the Church in Scotland was still very much out of touch with the Church on the Continent. Authorities abroad showed no interest in it and made no attempt to exercise jurisdiction over it, and it continued to walk in paths of its own.

Margaret of Scotland, Queen and Saint.—Not until the time of Queen Margaret and her family was the Scottish Church brought completely into conformity with the rest of the world. In this connection the year 1066 is important in Scottish history as well as in that of England. The Norman Conquest drove members of the dethroned royal family into exile, and thus the Princess Margaret found herself at the Scottish Court in Dunfermline, where she presently became the wife of King Malcolm Canmore.

Malcolm came to the throne in 1057 A.D. by defeating the usurper Macbeth whose name is familiar to us from Shakespere's tragedy. The territory over which he ruled was practically what is now Scotland without the islands in North and West. The king was an experienced soldier and must have profited by the years of exile which he spent in England, but he was far from being a man of culture, and his personality was nothing like so strong as that of his wife.

Margaret remains one of the most remarkable and influential figures in our national history. 'The Life of St Margaret' by Bishop Turgot (died 1115 A.D.) is an eulogy rather than a biography, but it leaves us convinced that she was a woman of unusual strength of character, intense religious fervour, and complete devotion to duty. She was sufficiently intelligent and educated to read the Bible and the works of the fathers in Latin, very strict and staid and serious, deeply concerned for the wellbeing of the Church and the people, interested in hermits and pilgrims, giving away in charity whatever she could find, even of her husband's property, washing the feet of beggars, ransoming English slaves, presenting rich vessels and embroidery to the churches. "Of all living persons whom I know or have known," says Turgot, "she was the most devoted to prayer and fasting, to works of mercy and almsgiving." She was an object of extreme reverence to all who knew her, including the king himself. Turgot reveals that Malcolm had "a sort of dread of offending her." As he could not read the books which she studied, he would turn them over with awe and kiss the covers, or have them ornamented with jewels for her. She certainly made his home more comfortable and his Court more dignified. Her virtue strikes us as somewhat self-conscious, and her nature as lacking in some of the more lovable human qualities, but she was a very conscientious mother and a most efficient queen and a powerful influence for good in the land.

It was with some horror that she discovered the peculiarities in Scottish religious practice, and she took in hand to have these reformed. She held repeated conferences with churchmen, and Turgot reports that: "Everything which she proposed she supported so strongly by the testimonies of the sacred Scriptures and the teaching of the holy Fathers that no one on the opposite side could say one word against them." Perhaps the most interesting point raised was that in Scotland many people hesitated about coming to Communion, fearing that they were unworthy, and might eat and drink judgment to themselves. "What!" said the Queen, "shall no one that is a sinner taste that Holy Mystery? If so, then it follows that no one at all should receive it, for no one is pure from sin . . . and if no one ought to receive it, why did the Lord make this proclamation in the Gospel: Except ye eat the flesh of the Son of Man and drink His blood, ye have no life in you ?" Non-churchgoing was another evil which she attempted to reform.

Queen Margaret died at Edinburgh Castle in 1093 A.D., her husband and eldest son having shortly before been killed while fighting against the English.

The Organisation of the Church in Scotland.—Her sons Alexander I. (reigned 1107-1124) and David I. (reigned 1124-1153) continued her work of bringing Scotland closer to the Church abroad. The Culdees, monks of an old Celtic type, originally hermits but latterly degenerate, were suppressed. The country was divided into dioceses or separate bishoprics (St Andrews, Moray, Dunkeld, Glasgow, Aberdeen, Ross, Caithness, Dunblane, Brechin). Later Scottish bishoprics were Galloway (under England till 1472), the Isles and Orkney (both under Norway till 1472), and Argyll (disjoined from Dunkeld about 1200). Each diocese had its cathedral, which contained the bishop's *cathedra* or chair. The bishop consecrated churches, ordained priests, and was the spiritual superior of his district. He was assisted at the cathedral by clergy called dean and canons, who formed the chapter, or governing body. He had certain judicial powers in connection with Canon or Church law. And besides this the work of a bishop included much that was of a semi-political nature, for such men, being better educated than the nobles, familiar with Latin, acquainted with other countries, and generally persons of mark, were very useful to the king as advisers and as ambassadors. Churchmen such as Bishop Lamberton of St Andrews, Bishop Elphinstone of Aberdeen, and Cardinal Beaton of St Andrews, like Wolsey in England and Richelieu in France, gave important service in connection with the government of the country.

The dioceses were composed of parishes, each with its priest, who would be called the rector or vicar and who would do all the work which we commonly expect of ministers of religion. In the Middle Ages preaching was not a task for which the ordinary priest was able, and it had to be done by the bishops or by visiting friars. The Greyfriars were founded by St Francis of Assisi in 1209, and the Blackfriars by St Dominic in 1220 A.D. The priest had his seven daily prayer 'hours' with the aid of his Breviary and daily Mass from the Missal, and for the people there was the regular Sunday service at which Mass (Communion) was celebrated. Children were baptised by the priest and confirmed by the bishop, marriages were solemnised, the confession of sins heard and absolution and penance pronounced, the sick visited and the distressed comforted, and extreme unction given to the dying, and funeral services were conducted. The people were taught to repeat the Lord's Prayer, the Apostles' Creed, and the Ten Commandments, to avoid the Seven Deadly Sins, to know the Seven Sacraments, the Seven Virtues, and the Seven Works of Mercy, to observe Christmas, Easter, and other sacred seasons and many Holy Days (called 'red-letter' days, because entered in red ink in the calendars) upon which saints were commemorated.

The religion of the people was superstitious, for they were ignorant and unable to read. Thus they regarded as of miraculous power the bones of dead saints, holy wells, pilgrimages, the sign of the Cross, images of the Virgin Mary and the saints, and prayers to saints, and, indeed, looked upon all religious ceremonies as magical. At the services they stood or knelt while the priests in their vestments went through the elaborate ritual which had developed in the course of the centuries. The service was all in Latin, and the people could not follow, but they could hear the sound of the priest's voice, see his reverent movements and the lights and vessels of the altar, smell the fragrant incense and feel the solemnity of the place and the occasion. They were at the stage when they required to be taught through the senses.

Alongside of the priests were the monks. Monasteries were favoured by Queen Margaret and her sons, but the monks who settled in the new abbeys were different from those of the Celtic period, and found their life-work, not in ministering to the people, but in spiritual exercises within the monastery for the saving of their own souls. Priests were called 'seculars,' while monks, because under a 'regula' or rule, were called 'regulars.' The monasteries were of various 'Orders,' some Benedictine (like Dunfermline), or belonging to the allied Cluniac (as Crossraguel) or Cistercian (as Newbattle) or Tironensian (as Arbroath) Orders; while others again were Augustinian (as Cambuskenneth). There were about 180 monastic houses of various sorts in Scotland, including those for monks, friars, nuns, templars, &c., and mostly founded in the twelfth and thirteenth centuries. The number of inmates in each of these institutions was not great, but an abbey such as Kelso was an extensive estate-owner, with many tenants on its farms and thousands of sheep. Monasteries helped the cause of civilisation, being peace-loving and socially useful. The monks were under a rule of 'obedience' to superiors, individual 'poverty,' and 'chastity' or purity of mind and action. They had their 'hours' in the chapel, ate together in the 'refectory,' met for business in the 'chapter-house,' chatted in the 'warming-room,' slept in the 'dormitory,' read or walked in the 'cloisters,' and, when sick, were tended in the 'infirmary.' Scottish monasteries do not seem to have had many books or to have done much for education, but much saintliness must have dwelt within these walls. Some also who were not able to face the rough world of those days took refuge in such institutions. In medieval times an ascetic life was highly esteemed, and it was imagined that one could not be a real Christian unless one left the world and took monastic vows. Such persons were therefore regarded as alone 'religious,' and when the word 'conversion' was used it referred to entering a monastery.

The Civilising Influence of the Church in Scotland.—The Middle Ages were accustomed to lawlessness, war, plague and famine, and knew little of science, progress, or comfort. But they had some compensations. One who loved that period has likened it to a rose-garden and modern times to a kitchen-garden. There were no machines, but this left room for skilled handwork. There was no swift transport, but people felt no need to rush about. A fascinating picture of the people of those leisurely times is to be found in Chaucer's 'Prologue.' Life was far from safe, and the fleetingness of the earthly was very clear, but this turned men's thoughts rather to the life hereafter. They had the hope of heaven and the fear of hell always with them. This explains some of the lavish generosity which made the Church wealthy. Of David I. it was said that—

> "He illumined in his days
> His lands with kirks and with abbeys,"

and he spent so much in this way that one of his descendants called him "a sore saint for the crown."

Art flourished in the Middle Ages. Painting, sculpture, music, wood-carving, architecture, embroidery, and the jeweller's craft were all the handmaids of religion. Scotland lagged behind most of Europe in development, but the period has left us something of its spirit in the cathedrals and abbeys. Many of them are in ruins now, chiefly because of war or neglect, but some have been carefully preserved or restored. A cathedral took a very long time to build, and there was often a change of plan or of circumstances, so that we find different styles of architecture together.

From the time of Queen Margaret, Norman influence was very strong in Scotland in all departments of life, and so we find the earlier churches Norman in style—

> "With massive arches, broad and round,
> That rose alternate, row on row,
> On ponderous columns, short and low."
>
> (Sir W. Scott, 'Marmion.')

This style we can see at Birnie, Leuchars, Dalmeny, St Margaret's Chapel in Edinburgh Castle, and the ruins of Dunfermline Abbey. Then came a movement towards what is termed Gothic, more graceful, with slender pillars, wider window spaces, delicate traceries, and supporting buttresses. Many of the most wonderful cathedrals of England and the Continent are Gothic. The Scottish cathedrals lie for the most part rather between these two styles which have been mentioned, and authorities speak of Transition and First-pointed styles in the cathedrals of St Andrews, Glasgow, Kirkwall, Dunblane, Elgin, Brechin, and such abbeys as Jedburgh, Arbroath, Holyrood, Pluscarden, Inchcolm. More truly Gothic is the later Melrose Abbey, of which Sir Walter Scott writes—

> "slender shafts of shapely stone,
> By foliaged tracery combined;
> Thou wouldst have thought some fairy's hand,
> Twixt poplars straight, the osier wand,
> In many a freakish knot has turned;
> Then framed a spell, when the work was done,
> And changed the willow-wreaths to stone."

Later still is the style of Paisley Abbey; Iona Cathedral; St John's Church, Perth; St Mary's Church, Biggar. The builders of the cathedrals and abbeys were generally foreign. King David I. "sent to France and Flanders and brought right crafty masons" to build Holyrood. We know of one mason from Paris who was employed at St Andrews, Glasgow, Melrose, and Paisley. About a hundred of the buildings at present in use as parish churches date from medieval times, and show some traces of their origin. Unfortunately the churches in those days were not all beautiful, any more than churches are to-day. The great majority were small and without interesting features, with earth floors and thatched roofs and the crudest decoration. But an impression of what was possible in Scotland may be gathered from Boece's account of King's College Church, Aberdeen, in the early sixteenth century:—

"There is a church floored with polished and squared stones, with windows, fine carved work, seats for the use of the priests, and benches for the boys, made with wonderful art; marble altars, images of the saints, statues and pictures gilt with gold; chairs of brass; hangings and carpets to cover the walls and floor, that the whole might appear more splendid. It was also magnificently decorated with much other precious furniture. The furnishings used for sacred functions consist of fifteen robes of cloth of gold, known as copes, chasubles, and tunics; and twenty-eight of a rough texture. All these were embroidered with a warp of golden threads, and had likenesses of the saints woven into them, the colours used being scarlet, purple, and blue. Seven of fine linen had palm leaves enwrought. These had fringes of linen threads, with golden stars scattered over them. Other twenty, also of linen, showed palm branches and a watered pattern. These were for the use of the boys in their sacred duties that their attendance on the priests might add to the dignity of the praise of God. Besides these, for every-day use there were many sacred vestments of scarlet cloth and watered linen. There were also a crucifix, two candlesticks, the same number of censers, an incense boat, six altar cruets, eight chalices, a textuary, two monstrances for holding the host, in which the body of Christ is carried round to be worshipped by the people, another of the same two cubits high of incredibly fine workmanship. Besides these were a finger-basin, a receptacle for water, a vessel for carrying round the holy water along with a sprinkler. All these were of gold and silver. There were also several cambric cloths, embroidered with gold and various figures, and others of the finest white linen, inwoven with flowers of various colour. With these the altars are covered in time of service. There, too, is a casquet of cypress-wood set with pearls and jewels, and of beautiful workmanship. In it are kept for worship the venerable relics of the saints set in gold and silver. The church has a bell-tower of immense height with a stone arch in the shape of an imperial crown, built with wonderful art and raised above the leaden roof. It contains thirteen bells, pleasing the ear with sweet and holy melody."

Books to read :—

Turgot, 'Life of St Margaret.' (Forbes-Leith's edition.)
J. Dowden, 'The Medieval Church in Scotland.' (1910.)
J. Stirling-Maxwell, 'Shrines and Homes of Scotland.' (1937.)

CHAPTER V.

THE PRE-REFORMATION CHURCH.

The Church 'Catholic' or Universal.—One thing to be noted about the Church in the Middle Ages is its Unity. We often complain to-day of the existence of so many kinds of Churches, and we support efforts towards Church Union because we realise that only by united witness can Christians hope to show forth adequately the spirit of Christ and meet successfully the anti-Christian influences which are so powerful in our world. In the medieval Church there were certainly differences, as, for example, amongst the various orders of monks, but there was at the same time a well-organised whole to which all Christians belonged.

The Church which God established in the world was one from the start. We call it the Body of Christ. It had "one Lord, one Faith, one Baptism, one God and Father of all" (Eph. iv. 5 and 6). But it was only by degrees that one visible Church with particular beliefs and practices came to be generally recognised. The Pope of Rome had, owing to various circumstances, come in the course of time to be acknowledged as the earthly head of this institution. His authority was something above the distinction of race from race. The Church used the one Latin language in all Western lands. The same Creeds were everywhere received. A common form of worship had slowly been introduced. Monks and friars and nuns felt equally at home in different countries. There was the same Church law (Canon Law) all over Western Europe. Had someone suddenly wakened up to discover himself in church there would have been little in the words of the service, the music of the organ, the chanting of the psalms, the sound of the church bells, the garments of the priests, the pictures on the walls, to tell him whether he was in Spain, Italy, France, Germany, or England. The headquarters of the Church at Rome were in touch with all parts of the known world. The Church provided the general framework of public and private life. "In the Middle Ages," says Professor W. M. Powicke, "the hold of the Church was due to the fact that it could satisfy the best cravings of the whole man, his love of beauty, his desire for goodness, his endeavour after truth."

The authority of the Church had much increased as the centuries passed. The only way of salvation was now believed to be through the sacraments which were under the control of the Church. Kings, nobles, and peasants alike feared to offend the Church, and the most wicked people were as eager as any by gifts and vows to avoid its disfavour.

The authority of the Church dictated men's beliefs, and a traditional theology had been built up which was very far from what was familiar in the first centuries after Christ. There were learned European theologians in the Middle Ages, the greatest being Thomas Aquinas (died 1274 A.D.). Another was Duns Scotus (died 1308 A.D.) who may have been born in the South of Scotland, and the disdainful use of whose name by his opponents has given us the word 'dunce.' The doctrine which came to be imposed in those days required acceptance of Transubstantiation (the replacing of the substance of the bread and wine in Communion by the body and blood of Christ), Purgatory (a state in which the souls of the dead are cleansed by suffering), compulsory celibacy (forbidding clergy to marry), Seven Sacraments (Baptism, Confirmation, Eucharist, Penance, Orders, Marriage, Extreme Unction), the value of external works (confession to a priest, penance, pilgrimages, &c.), and Mariolatry (worship of the Virgin Mary).

The learned in the universities which the Church had done so much to found discussed and disputed over such matters. The great mass of the people, however, were extremely ignorant, unable to read or write, or express themselves or grasp difficult ideas. That was why the Church put more and more display into its services. Pictures, statues, lights, bells, vestments, incense, oil, holy water, processions, gestures, organs, banners, relics were calculated to impress simple people. Anyone could at least remember what he saw, whether or not he understood it. Additions were made to the old simple services (for example, in Baptism) to teach new lessons and to make the occasions more memorable. But when one starts this process there is no reason why one should ever stop, and the services became overgrown with extras and the original meaning was almost smothered. The people were also fed, not so much on the Bible as on legends about saints, and these were often childish stories without any foundation. Here, again, the idea was to teach through concrete example, and to lead men to admire the qualities of holy persons and imitate them.

The Church in the World.—The Church in those days as the one great supernational authority was a kind of medieval United Nations Council. It offered the common ground upon which all races might meet. Very naturally, however, it tended to take advantage of its position and became overriding and tyrannical. Political and worldly matters assumed a prominent place among its interests. We have all several loyalties, as, for example, that which we owe to our family and that which we owe to the State. They do not necessarily conflict, but they may. In the Middle Ages the Pope and his government had the first call upon the loyalty of priests, monks, nuns, and others set apart by the Church, and the Pope could contrive the appointment of men to bishoprics in this or that country with a view to their being his agents rather than first of all concerned for the country where they were to work. The Church was a sort of super-State whose interests were not necessarily those of the people of the land. The doctrine of the Sovereignty of God, the place which religion had occupied in the kingdoms of Israel and Judah, and the teaching of St Augustine's famous book, 'The City of God,' encouraged the Church to claim a controlling position over kings and nations.

As a matter of fact, instead of being above political differences, it inclined to become itself just another political power, as, for example, in connection with the Scottish fight for Independence.

The Church sought, not only to have political supremacy, but to control every department of life and activity. Up to a point it did splendid service, for it kept certain ideals alive in the world. Thus in that wild period its monasteries, wisely guided, could be, as it were, hothouses in which beautiful flowers of piety might be safely reared. They unquestionably did something to preserve religion and save it from being paganised and possibly destroyed in those rough times.

The Church provided the necessary encouragement for education. It was the founder of schools, the trainer of teachers, the producer and the guardian of manuscripts. It gave its patronage to the Seven Liberal Arts (grammar, rhetoric, dialectic, arithmetic, geometry, music, and astronomy). It originated and staffed the universities. Scotland owes the universities of St Andrews, Glasgow, and Aberdeen to the pre-Reformation Church.

It was the Church that conserved the spirit of Charity through the Middle Ages. The care of the poor and the provision of hospitals were left to it. There was much suffering as a result of war and disease, and there was much unemployment; and such evils the Church was able to moderate, though not to prevent nor to cure.

At the same time the very range of the Church's interest and activities brought with it the temptation to forget that it is the Gospel that is the power of God unto Salvation.

The Church and Scottish Independence.—Although the medieval Church in Scotland was part of this great body of which we have been speaking, and although it long held without question what was thus generally accepted throughout Christendom, it was able to show a decided spirit of independence within the unity.

This came out in connection with the unsuccessful attempt of the Church in England to include Scotland within its territory. Both the Archbishop of Canterbury and the Archbishop of York claimed Scotland, and the fact of this dispute between them had something to do with Scotland's escape from both. The Scottish Church leaders in the time of Alexander I. (1107-1124 A.D.) had occasion to assert their independence. The matter became serious again in the reign of William the Lion (1165-1214). In 1174 this Scottish monarch was captured by the English and forced to become a vassal of King Henry II., and the treaty between the two countries at this time declared that "the Church of England should have that authority in the Church of Scotland which by right it ought to have"—a phrase which Canterbury, York, and Scotland all interpreted differently. In 1189 Richard I. of England gave up his rights under this treaty in return for a money payment. Successive Popes took somewhat different attitudes towards the Scottish Church. At one time William the Lion quarrelled so seriously with the Pope over the choice of a bishop for St Andrews that Scotland was placed under an interdict, that is to say, deprived of all sacraments and religious services for the time being. But Pope Clement III. in 1188 issued a bull (so called from the leaden seal or 'bulla' attached to the document) which declared the Scottish Church to be the "special daughter" of Rome "none intervening"; a decision afterwards confirmed by other Popes. From 1225 the Scottish Church was allowed to hold Councils of its own for the regulation of its affairs. Although the independence of the Scottish Church was thus admitted, it was not until 1472 that the first archbishop was appointed in Scotland. Latterly not only St Andrews but also Glasgow was granted this dignity.

Alexander III. (1249-1286 A.D.) showed strong objection to anything like undue papal interference in Scotland, and on occasion encouraged the Scottish clergy to ignore instructions which came from Rome. During the Wars of Independence under Sir William Wallace and Robert Bruce, Scottish relations with the Papacy were unfriendly. The Pope in a far from impartial and supernational spirit actively sided with England in this long and fierce struggle. The Scottish Church retaliated by giving no heed to his messages and orders. Contributions which would ordinarily have gone to Rome remained uncollected. A summons to four Scottish bishops to appear before the Pope in 1320 was calmly disregarded. Only when at last in 1328 the independence of Scotland and the sovereignty of Robert Bruce were formally recognised, did Scotland admit once more its allegiance to the Pope.

During the period of struggle the country was in much too serious a plight for affairs in the Church to be well ordered or prosperous. But its spirit was by no means exhausted. There can be no doubt as to the importance of the contribution it had meanwhile made to the cause of Scottish independence. Bishop Lamberton of St Andrews (died 1328 A.D.) and Bishop

Wishart of Glasgow (died 1316 A.D.) proved themselves conspicuous patriots, and others dared greatly in support of Bruce. "Ah, Freedom is a noble thing," sings the poet Barbour as the key-note of this critical time. Scotland deliberately chose independence with poverty, and the Church of Scotland shares the responsibility for this choice.

Activities of the Church in Scotland.—In the period of the early Stuarts there were other problems. Scotland suffered almost continuously from rebellion, invasion, assassination, burning, theft, intrigue, pestilence, poverty. James I. and James III. were murdered. The deaths of James II., James IV., and James V. were all premature and connected with the struggle against England. Royalty was not very plainly exalted above nobility, and nobles were often turbulent. Regencies when monarchs were mere children or prisoners in England were a source of suspicion and jealousy. It was a royal prince who in a personal quarrel burnt Elgin Cathedral in 1390. It was English troops that set fire to the abbeys of Newbattle, Dryburgh, and Melrose in 1385. Kelso Jedburgh, Melrose, Dryburgh were eventually destroyed by the English in 1545. Defeats of Scottish troops such as that of Nelville's Cross (1346) and that of Flodden (1513) added to the country's sorrows.

There was, however, a bright side. Scotland kept in touch with the Continent, especially through the long-standing alliance with France, which left permanent traces on Scottish life and language. Many Scots widened their experience by service abroad. The Stuarts, too, had their ideals. James I. longed to make Scotland safe for its people so that, to use his own words, the key would keep the castle, and the broom bush the cow. James IV. had an Act of Parliament passed in 1496 to compel men in good position to send their eldest sons to grammar schools to learn Latin thoroughly.

In this age also the Scottish burghs, especially on the east coast, were developing through foreign trade, and there from an early date good schools were to be found, taught by churchmen. The universities of St Andrews (1411 A.D.), Glasgow (1451), and Aberdeen (1494) were founded on the lines of those at Paris and Bologna.

The Church showed some enterprise in the establishment of the collegiate churches. About forty of these were erected, chiefly in the fifteenth century. They were not parish churches, but larger, and with a staff of clergy almost like that of a small cathedral, and they were meant to be special centres of religious devotion and instruction. It was an experiment which showed that there was life and zeal in the Church. The collegiate churches included St Mary's, Biggar; St Giles's, Edinburgh; Crail; Lincluden; Bothwell; Cullen; Dunbar; St Duthac's, Tain; St Nicholas's, Aberdeen; and others.

Scottish religion in this period was strengthened by several notable men amongst its leaders. James Kennedy, Bishop of St Andrews (died 1465 A.D.), grandson of King Robert III., deserves to be remembered as a man of outstanding character, piety, liberality, learning, and statesmanship. Of him Spottiswoode the historian says: "He did put all things in such order as no man then living did remember to have seen the Church in so good an estate." Upon his sagacity and prudence James II. depended in all serious political situations.

William Elphinstone, Bishop of Aberdeen (died 1514 A.D.), was another churchman of sterling merit. He studied at Glasgow and abroad, and became highly skilled in Church Law. Both James III. and James IV. found him a trustworthy ambassador to foreign courts and a faithful adviser in State affairs. His interest in the education and spiritual training of his clergy is shown by his foundation of King's College, Aberdeen. He did much to improve the buildings at his cathedral, and was responsible for the production of the Aberdeen Breviary, a service book which was amongst the earliest of Scottish printed works. When he died at the age of eighty-two he left a high reputation as a religious man, of blameless life, a hard worker, fond of books, given to hospitality, patriotic in spirit.

Books to read :—

A. Mure Mackenzie, 'Robert Bruce.' (1934.)
A. Mure Mackenzie, 'The Rise of the Stewarts.' (1935.)
A. R. MacEwen, 'A History of the Church in Scotland.' (1913, 1918.)

CHAPTER VI.

THE DAWN OF THE REFORMATION.

The End of the Middle Ages.—Sometimes a system is successful for a while and then breaks down. The blessings which it produces at first outweigh any disadvantages which it may involve. But presently conditions change. The disadvantages begin to outbalance the blessings. And soon the system has to give place to one that will better satisfy new circumstances.

Thus the medieval Church served a high purpose in its day. In a lawless time it provided a refuge for religion and culture in its monasteries. In an uneducated age it provided ceremonies, pictures, and images—the books of the unlearned. In a period of superstition, it fostered outward practices and developed new doctrines. In days when standards were low and civil law in a crude state, the Church encouraged the gentler virtues and by its Canon Law set the tone for the nations. In times when there was yet little national consciousness, it provided something like unity. In a world situation where authority prevailed everywhere, it saw that the Church had the controlling place in man's life.

But a critical moment in world history had been reached. This happens now and again, as it certainly did at the beginning of the Christian era, and as perhaps it is doing once again in our day. The Reformation period saw a very complete change in human outlook, and as a consequence monasteries, ceremonies, doctrinal novelties, mere outward works, a church enriched by pious donors, papal supremacy, ecclesiastical law, clerical control of politics, and of the means of salvation, no longer had the same justification.

Social changes had taken place. The northern countries

of Europe had gradually been overtaking the southern in civilisation, and were now all the more important since the Church had lost its hold in the Near East, first through the rise of Mohammedanism (Mohammed died in 632 A.D.) and then through the secession from Roman communion of the whole Eastern Church in 1054 A.D., and finally through the advance of the Turks, who captured Constantinople in 1453 A.D.

There were new trade developments; people in towns were better off and more independent; they had discovered a bigger world by the help of Columbus and Vasco da Gama. Even the peasants had a new sense of power since feudal conditions were failing, and gunpowder enabled them at last to face the armoured knight. A new national patriotism was appearing, and an interest in national languages had begun.

There were also great intellectual changes. Such teaching as that of Copernicus (died 1543 A.D.), that our earth was not after all the centre of the universe, drove men to question the voice of authority and tradition. Education and scholarship and individual thinking progressed. Interest was revived in old literature; and the Hebrew and Greek of the Bible were once more examined. The invention of printing was of incalculable and epoch-making importance.

Further, there were spiritual and moral changes. We notice a demand for less external and more real, inward, personal religion. Men found that it was not enough to go through certain performances; one must mean what one was doing; one must have faith. The individual was becoming more self-conscious, and discovering that he could in fact go direct to God without a priest, and that it was the Grace of God rather than the authority of the Church that should concern him. Thus he obtained freedom from the stranglehold which the Church had on everyone through its claim to be the only medium of salvation. The layman began to feel himself entitled to take a share in Church affairs. The appearance of the Bible in the language of the people made a great difference. Tyndale's English translation of the New Testament was published in 1526. Luther's German Bible was complete by 1534. People at once wanted to have this wonderful rediscovered book explained, and this required far more preaching than there had been. From the Bible they soon learned that the Church had wandered sadly from the faith once revealed to the Apostles.

Again, the new conditions of living led men to the conviction that they could after all be Christians in ordinary occupations and without leaving the world and going into monasteries.

People were also growing more sensitive about abuses prevailing within the Church. These included the worldly lives of Popes and higher clergy, the disproportionate wealth of the Church at a time when peasants were becoming awake to their oppressed condition and when the nobles were no longer so rich as they had been; the obsession of Church leaders with political matters when they were not any more the only educated persons available for political positions; the immoral living of many monks and friars; the lamentable ignorance of the lower clergy who were in charge of the parishes; the heavy death-duties and other exactions of the churchmen; evils with regard to the making of appointments to high places in the Church; bribery with a view to office (simony); holding more than one full-time appointment (pluralities); appointing friends apart from any qualification (nepotism); giving important posts to mere children that they might have an income; and so on. The Church had indeed become very corrupt, and was felt not to be now providing men with the Word that they needed or conveying to them the power that they required; and it seemed incapable of adapting itself to the new world conditions.

The New Age.—Hence the Reformation. From time to time attempts had already been made to improve things in the Church. Thus John Wiclif (died 1384 A.D.), a learned Oxford don, went back to Scripture teaching, and would have liked to restore the Church to what it was before wealth and politics and superstition corrupted it. His disciple, John Hus, in Prague was burned to death in 1415 for similar views. A like fate befell that dark-eyed, excitable Dominican friar, Savonarola, at Florence in 1498. By his marvellous power as a preacher he produced a religious and moral revival, pointing back to the early Church by contrast with that of Italy in his day. In England, the spirit of the Renaissance (or New Birth) was introduced by Thomas More (died 1535), the tragic Lord Chancellor, one of the finest characters of his time; and by his friend John Colet (died 1519), Dean of St Paul's, London, who influenced many by his fresh expositions of St Paul's Epistles. Erasmus of Rotterdam (died 1536) was perhaps the greatest of all the forerunners of the Reformation. His scholarly work on the Greek New Testament, his personal devoutness as we see it in his 'Handbook of the Christian Soldier,' and his scathing criticisms of the churchmen of the day in his 'Praise of Folly' and some of his 'Colloquies' made him a powerful agent for reform.

But the real outbreak of the Reformation in Europe dates from 31st October 1517 when Martin Luther (1483-1546 A.D.) nailed up his Theses at Wittenberg in Germany denouncing certain abuses. He was an Augustinian monk, a man of genuine religious experience, with a profound knowledge of the Bible and the works of the Fathers. By his strong human personality, his courage, his numerous writings, his translation of the Bible, his popular hymns, his message of Justification by Faith and the Priesthood of all Believers, he did more than any other to revive Christianity. John Calvin (1509-1564 A.D.) issued the first edition of his 'Institutes' in 1536, and set up in Geneva a system of reformed doctrine, worship, and discipline which became the model for the Protestantism of France, Holland, Hungary, Scotland, America, and elsewhere. Calvin was a cultured gentleman, reserved and cold in manner, a lawyer by training, a master of logic and system, a clear writer, a skilful administrator, a stern Puritan, a man of commanding will. He specially emphasised the doctrine of the Sovereignty of God. John Knox found Calvin's Geneva "the most perfect school of Christ that ever was in the earth since the days of the Apostles."

The Reformation movement was effective in Germany and the Scandinavian countries, France, Holland, Bohemia, Hungary, England, and influenced other lands. The most important efforts to stop its progress were the foundation of the Jesuit Order (Society of Jesus) by Ignatius Loyola in 1540 and the decisions of the Romanist Council of Trent (1545-1563).

Scotland hears of the Reformation.—The Scottish Reformation was part of the general movement. John Resby, an English priest, had been burned at Perth in 1406;

and Paul Crawer, a follower of John Hus, was similarly treated at St Andrews in 1433, while in 1494 some thirty persons known as the Lollards of Kyle were charged with Wiclifite heresy.

But the first Scottish martyr of the Reformation was Patrick Hamilton (1503-1528), a talented youth, of a distinguished family, who became infected with the new ideas whilst a student in Paris and Louvain, and who later went to the reformed University of Marburg in Germany, where he submitted Theses ('Patrick's Places') and proved himself "a man of excellent learning and very acute mind," a man whose "judgment in divine truth was eminently clear and solid." His evangelical spirit appears in his words: "O how ready would we be to help others, if we knew His goodness and gentleness toward us. He is a good and gentle Lord and He does all things for nought. Let us, I beseech you, follow His footsteps, whom all the world ought to praise and worship." His grip of Reformation principles is plain from such an utterance as this: "Thou must do good works, but beware that thou do them not to deserve any good through them." When Hamilton returned to his native land in 1527 he deliberately set about the proclamation of the Gospel. As Knox puts it: "The bright beams of the true light which by God's grace was planted in his heart, began most abundantly to burst forth as well in public as in secret." But it was only for a very few months that he had liberty to exercise his gifts. He was invited to St Andrews (where he had once been a student) and the archbishop permitted him to expound his views; but it was only that what he said might be used in evidence against him, and on 29th February 1528 he was tried, condemned as a heretic, and burned before St Salvator's College. This piece of persecution attracted attention to Hamilton's teaching, and it was said that if others were to be put to death it would have to be in underground cellars, since "the reek of Patrick Hamilton had infected all it blew upon."

In other ways knowledge of the Reformation had been reaching Scotland. We hear that some people in Aberdeen had books by Luther, and were impressed by his opinions, while merchants at St Andrews and Leith sold copies of Tyndale's New Testament which they had smuggled from the

Continent. Acts of Parliament were unavailing to stop the distribution of such literature, and in 1543 Parliament was actually persuaded to permit the use of an English translation of the Bible. In telling of this occasion, John Knox says: "Then might have been seen the Bible lying almost upon every gentleman's table. The New Testament was borne about in many men's hands."

That the seriousness of the abuses in the Church was widely recognised is evident from the poems of Sir David Lyndsay (died 1555), Lord Lyon King of Arms, and the reception given to his play, 'A Pleasant Satire of the Three Estates,' when performed before James V. at Linlithgow in 1540. Lyndsay shows the place which the New Testament in English was taking in people's interest, the public contempt for unworthy monks and nuns and inefficient and worldly priests, the discontent aroused by the Church's constant demands for money, the widespread desire for preaching and religious instruction, the hostility of general opinion with regard to the evils associated with confession to a priest, with unscriptural doctrines such as that of Purgatory, with the trade in relics, and with the many superstitious practices which the Church had been encouraging. Speaking of Lyndsay, Sir Walter Scott refers to—

> "The flash of that satiric rage,
> Which, bursting on the early stage,
> Branded the vices of the age
> And broke the keys of Rome."

The 'Good and Godly Ballads' collected by the brothers Wedderburn were described by one of the Reformers as amongst the "more particular means whereby many in Scotland got some knowledge of God's truth in the time of great darkness." They included metrical psalms, Lutheran hymns, and popular songs with religious references and with Reformation teaching.

The Price of Progress.—Sympathy with the new movement was increased through the work of George Wishart (1512-1546). As a schoolmaster in Montrose he took up the study of the Greek New Testament. Later in Switzerland, Germany, and England he strengthened his Reformation convictions, and, returning to Scotland, preached at Dundee and elsewhere. He is described as tall, dark-haired, long-bearded, courteous in manner, simple in his way of living, very charitable, an earnest teacher. His activities were soon cut short. By order of Cardinal David Beaton he was arrested and taken to St Andrews, where outside the castle he was burned at the stake on 1st March 1546. One of those who had been interested in Wishart's message and had accompanied him in the Lothians was John Knox. On the night of his arrest Wishart had sent Knox away, saying with gloomy foreboding, " One is sufficient for a sacrifice."

Meantime the cause had had other martyrs whose names are recorded by Knox, the most interesting being Thomas Forret (1538), a scholarly priest at Dollar, who had proved himself a devoted and kindly pastor and a faithful preacher of the Gospel. The last to suffer death for Reformation principles was an aged priest named Walter Milne (1558). To escape a like fate other pious and learned men were obliged to leave their native land. One of these, Alesius (1500-1565), attained distinction as a university teacher in Germany, while another, Macchabæus (died 1557), became a tower of strength to the reformed Church in Denmark.

These cases of persecution, though not so many as in most countries, show that the Church leaders realised the seriousness of the opposition which they had roused. Provincial Councils of churchmen in 1549, 1552, and 1559 made many regulations with a view to removing scandals and abuses. The transactions of these assemblies fully expose the rottenness of the Church. Unfortunately good resolutions proved of no effect; and it is difficult to see how a real change for the better could have been achieved while control of the Church remained in the hands of men so devoid of Christian principles as Cardinal Beaton and Archbishop Hamilton.

David Beaton (1494-1546) by ability, personality, education, and experience became Scotland's greatest ecclesiastical statesman. His interests were almost entirely secular and political; but in that period of intrigue he showed more real patriotism than most of his countrymen. He was immoral and unscrupulous, and, although he actively resisted the Reformers, he did nothing to improve the conditions which roused their zeal. Shortly after the death of Wishart, a plot was laid against the cardinal, and he was murdered in his castle of St Andrews. Even his worst enemies admitted that—

> "Although the loon was well away
> The deed was foully done."

John Hamilton (1512-1571), who succeeded to the archbishopric, was a prelate of even more dissolute habits, and altogether of a weaker and more self-seeking type. He was, however, responsible for the issue of what is called 'Hamilton's Catechism' (1551), an extremely interesting and valuable document intended to meet the demand for fuller instruction in religious truth, and setting forth in simple fashion the Commandments, the Creed, the Seven Sacraments, and the Lord's Prayer; but this work appeared too late to have any effect in stemming the tide of Reformation feeling.

Books to read :—

D. Hay Fleming, 'The Reformation in Scotland.' (1910.)
A. F. Mitchell, 'The Scottish Reformation.' (1900.)
T. M. Lindsay, 'A History of the Reformation.' (1906.)

CHAPTER VII.

THE WORK OF JOHN KNOX.

The Early Life of Knox.—The great monument of the Reformation at Geneva shows such figures and names as those of Luther, Calvin, Beza, William the Silent, Cromwell, and John Knox. As the representative of the Scottish Reformation none other than Knox could have been chosen. Froude declares that amongst British Reformers "no grander figure can be found than that of Knox." Thomas Carlyle has called him "the one Scotchman to whom his country and the world owe a debt."

John Knox was born near Haddington in 1515, early in the reign of James V. His people were not well off, but were able to give him the necessary training for the priesthood, and when we first hear of him he was acting as tutor in a laird's household. The families with which he came into contact at this time were interested in Reformation ideas as reported from England, and Knox's sympathies were in the same direction when George Wishart arrived in the district in 1546. Knox attached himself openly to Wishart, and had the honour of carrying a two-handed sword which was evidently thought necessary for the Reformer's protection as he moved about the country on his perilous mission.

After Wishart had been burned and the cardinal murdered, we again hear of Knox. He arrived with his young charges at the castle of St Andrews which the Protestants had seized, and where many who felt themselves in danger from the persecutors had now gathered. John Knox speedily attracted attention by his Protestant zeal and his skill in discussion, and one Sunday in the parish church the minister from the pulpit publicly called upon him to give himself to the work of a preacher. Thereafter he preached and taught ardently and faithfully till French troops attacked and captured the castle, when he was carried off to serve as a slave at the oars of a French warship. One day from his place in the galley he saw the steeple of Holy Trinity Church, St Andrews, where he had first preached, and he expressed the conviction that he would live to preach there again in better times. After a year and a half of this sore and humiliating experience, peace with France gave him his release. He was sent back to England, and the situation in Scotland being still most unfavourable, settled in the border town of Berwick, and for some years exercised a successful ministry there. Those were the days of Edward VI., when, under the inspiration of Cranmer, the Reformation movement was progressing rapidly. Knox became well known to the leading English churchmen, was appointed one of the King's chaplains, and was even offered a bishopric. Amongst the friends of Reform in England there were already two parties, one interested in retaining as much as possible of what had been of value in the pre-Reformation Church, the other anxious to remove as much as possible of what had been corrupt and unhealthy. Knox sided with the latter and was a real strength to them. He is credited with obtaining the insertion of what was called the 'black rubric' in the English prayer book—an explanation that though kneeling at Communion was practised it implied no 'adoration,' and therefore no acceptance of the Romish doctrine of Transubstantiation.

In 1553 Mary succeeded her half-brother Edward VI. on the throne of England. She was a fervent Romanist and Knox and many more found it necessary to flee the country. After a short stay in Dieppe he went to Switzerland and visited several of the leaders of the Reformation movement there, and for the first time met John Calvin, the Reformer of Geneva, whose devoted admirer he was ever to remain. At this time there were many English in exile for conscience' sake, and in 1554 Knox accepted charge of a congregation of these at Frankfort in Germany. Here, however, the difference of outlook between the two types of English Protestant soon showed itself, and when presently the more ritualistic party gained the upper hand, Knox had to leave. He returned to Geneva and took over the ministry of an English congregation there, where his ideas were more acceptable. In the latter part of 1555, however, we find him on a visit to Scotland. There he was much surprised at the extent and depth of the Reformation interest which revealed itself in many quarters. His memories of the Scotland which he had left a few years before had not led him to expect such "fervent thirst," such "groaning for the bread of life." The sagacious Erskine of Dun, the courageous preacher John Willock, the rising politician Maitland of Lethington, James Stewart, who was to be the Regent Moray, the able and intelligent Earl of Glencairn, were representative of a cause that was by no means hopeless, and a movement that was by no means negligible.

Knox stayed for some nine months in Scotland, preaching and celebrating Communion in the Mearns, in Ayrshire, in the Lothians and elsewhere. Perhaps his chief influence was in convincing those who desired the purity and simplicity of Bible Christianity that they must now break with the existing Church organisation as an idolatrous and anti-Christian institution. When he returned to Geneva he left behind him such a reputation for infectious enthusiasm that as time went on the Protestant leaders more and more felt that he was the one man whom Scotland needed, and a deputation went to Geneva with a call which was so pressing that Calvin and others assured Knox that he could not refuse it, "unless he would declare himself rebellious unto his God and unmerciful to his country." As things fell out, it was not till 2nd May 1559 that Knox actually reached Scotland.

By this date Knox had gathered wide experience. He had had valuable contacts with English, German, Swiss, and French Reformers and congregations. But, in particular, he had been closely associated for some years with John Calvin and with the Church organised by him at Geneva. Knox called Calvin "that singular instrument of God." In doctrine, worship, and government Calvin based his system always upon what his study of the Bible led him to believe was the mind of Christ. Hence his emphasis on the Sovereignty of God. Hence a form of worship stripped of ceremony, the chief new interest being in the congregational singing of metrical psalms, which had been carefully taught to the children, and the faithful instruction of the people through the sermon. Under his form of Church government laymen were given a real place in the rule of the congregation, and bishops were rejected as bringing with them State-control and clerical tyranny.

Knox accepted the general position of Calvin as truly biblical; and the Church which he eventually organised in Scotland was meant to be a return to early Christianity, with a complete rejection of all ideas and practices which had been added by men in later centuries without scriptural justification. Knox said: "Whatsoever He approveth by His eternal word, that shall be approved, and whatsoever He condemneth, shall be condemned."

The Reformation Conflict in Scotland.—The movement for Reform in Scotland had been strengthening. Scotland and France had an "auld alliance," whilst Scotland and England had only too frequently been enemies. The English had won at Flodden in 1513, at Pinkie in 1547, and destructive English raids had been common. Mary of Scots, the child Queen (born 1542), had therefore been sent to France and married to the future French king, Francis II.

But the French party was over-zealous. Mary of Guise, who acted latterly as regent for her youthful daughter, was thoroughly French in outlook and ambitions, and the danger that Scotland would presently be no more than an outlying province of the French kingdom became serious. To be ruled by France was not the same as to be allied with France, and, as a result, Scottish good-feeling towards England increased. The Protestants in particular inclined to look to Protestant England for assistance. As Mary of Guise could not for a time afford to offend or alarm this party, she was obliged to be tolerant of them, and consequently they became bolder and more numerous.

The regent was clever but unscrupulous, and eventually the Protestants altogether lost faith in her, and when Knox landed in Scotland he found what was practically a state of civil war. For a time the regent with her trained French soldiers had the best of the struggle; but she died in the summer of 1559, and when Queen Elizabeth, who was now ruling in England, at last sent an army into Scotland in support of the Protestants, the French were forced to abandon their hopes and leave the country.

The Lords of the Congregation, as the Protestant leaders were called, now controlled Scotland. They included the men who had pledged themselves some years before to "maintain, set forward, and establish the most blessed Word of God and His congregation," and who had renounced Romish superstition and had declared their resolve that in every parish Protestant services should be held, and that "doctrine, preaching, and interpretation of Scriptures be had and used privately in quiet houses, without great conventions of the people thereto, till God move the prince to grant public preaching by faithful and true ministers."

Knox, since his arrival, had been assiduously and vehemently stirring the people from the pulpit. He was peculiarly gifted for such work. His passionate conviction, his command of Bible language, his talent for effective denunciation, his voice, his look, his gestures, and, more than anything else, his forceful character and personality made his preaching irresistible. The crowds were carried away by his oratory. "The voice of that one man," it was said, "is able to put more life in us in one hour than five hundred trumpets blustering in our ears."

There was plenty of discontent in those days, but it was Knox who turned it into a channel that was religious, rather than merely political or social. He was indeed held by some to be "too extreme," and to "strike at the root." He certainly had no love for compromise or half-measures. But it is important to insist that the Reformation was a Reformation, and that its very complete success was the work, not of self-seeking conspirators and lawless mobs, but of one who could be thus described by a personal friend: "A man of God, the light of Scotland, the comfort of the Church, the mirror of godliness and pattern and example to all true ministers in purity of life, soundness of doctrine, and boldness in reproving of wickedness."

There were nobles who keenly supported a movement which they calculated would enrich them with lands that had belonged to the Church. There were mobs whose hatred of the clerical oppression under which they had suffered, and whose contempt for the low morals of those who had called themselves 'religious,' could apparently find no better means of expression than the raiding of monasteries and the destruction of statues, woodwork, books, and ornaments. Hence the damage at Perth, Scone, St Andrews, and elsewhere. All who assisted in the attack upon the old bad ways were not necessarily eager to be led to new and better ways. But Knox saw to it that there were set before the people in those days fresh spiritual ideals and fresh spiritual opportunities. The Reformation as it took hold of more and more of the earnest folks of Scotland, meant the devout reading of the Bible, the singing of psalms, the guidance of morals by pious and experienced elders from among the people themselves, the preaching of the Gospel in language that could be understood, and by men who could be respected, the knowledge that men were called by God to serve Him in their own station, and that Salvation comes by sincere Faith in the heart.

The Church Reformed.—There was much to be done before the Church could indeed be called Reformed. Meanwhile Parliament officially abolished the use of the Latin Mass, rejected the Episcopal system, approved a Confession of Faith which set forth the teaching accepted by the Reformers, encouraged Knox to state his views as to Church government, education, and other important practical matters, and issued for the guidance of the worship of God Knox's 'Liturgy' or 'Book of Common Order.'

The Scots Confession was adopted in 1560 as "wholesome and sound doctrine grounded upon the infallible truth of God's Word." It was the work of a Committee of six ministers, all of whom happen to have had the same Christian name, John Knox, John Row, John Spottiswoode, John Winram, John Douglas, and John Willock, who put it together in the course of a few days on the lines of other Reformed statements of the Faith, and especially the teaching of Calvin in his 'Institutes.'

There is an interesting statement in the Preface: "If any man will note in this our Confession any article or sentence repugnant to God's Holy Word, that it would please him of his gentleness and for Christian charity's sake to admonish us of the same in writing; and we upon our honours and fidelity by God's grace do promise unto him satisfaction from the mouth of God, that is from His Holy Scriptures, or else reformation of that which he shall prove to be amiss." According to the Scots Confession, the marks of a true Church are the true preaching of the Word, the right administration of the Sacraments, and discipline uprightly ministered. This Confession was never supposed to take the place of the Apostles' Creed, which every child was expected to know; but it was meant to be a fuller explanation of the Church's beliefs, and especially to insist upon points which Romanism had obscured or confused. It has been described as "the warm utterance of a people's heart." It was more a manifesto for the moment than a complete theology, and it is not surprising that in calmer days it was found desirable to replace it by the more careful and elaborate Westminster Confession of 1647.

The Scots Confession was the Confession of Faith, not only of Knox and Melville and the Covenanting Alexander Henderson, but also of the Scottish Episcopalians of the early seventeenth century, and some later churchmen have spoken highly of it, including Edward Irving and John Macleod Campbell. The Scots Confession was described officially in connection with the Church Union of 1929 as "held in honour as having an important place in the history of Scottish Presbyterianism."

The First Book of Discipline was the work of the same Committee. It did not receive Parliamentary approval, being regarded by some as "devout imaginings" and requiring the provision of more money than it was convenient to put at the disposal of the Church; but it explained the Church's proposals with regard to the practical management of spiritual affairs. It was superseded in 1581 by the Second Book of Discipline, which has since remained the basis of Church practice.

In the First Book of Discipline there is guidance for simple celebration of Baptism and Communion, as well as for Sunday and week-day service, for the temporary appointment of readers to take charge of parishes until ministers could be trained in sufficient numbers, for the election of qualified ministers agreeable to the people, for selecting a few outstanding men as superintendents to supervise the whole work of the ministers and readers, for a very enlightened policy of national education, for the annual electing of "men of best knowledge of God's Word and cleanest life" as elders and deacons to look after the behaviour of the people and to provide for the poor. One clause requires that "every church have a Bible in English and that the people be commanded to convene to hear the plain reading or interpretation of the Scriptures." People are urged to practise singing the psalms. Family worship is commended. The religious knowledge of the parishioners is to be periodically examined. Ministers are to meet regularly for Scripture study. Like Calvin, Knox would have had fairly frequent Communion celebrations, but four times a year is what is here suggested, only those to be admitted who knew the Apostles' Creed, the Lord's Prayer, and the Ten Commandments. The Lord's Day is to be strictly observed.

The Book of Common Order became the rule of worship in 1564, and continued in use until the issue of the Directory for the Public Worship of God in 1645, and again, under the Second Episcopate in the seventeenth century. The Second Prayer Book of Edward VI. (1552) had been employed before Knox, on the basis of his Geneva experience, produced this new form of prayers which is first mentioned in the First Book of Discipline. Stress was laid upon following the liturgy in the celebration of the Sacraments and of marriage, and guidance was provided for the order and content of the regular services. When services were conducted by readers, the prescribed wording was closely followed, but ministers were encouraged to use their own prayers. The Book of Common Order was helpful as a guide to "the substance and right ordering of all the parts of divine worship." The ordinary service consisted of a call to worship, a prayer of confession and supplication for pardon, a metrical psalm, a short prayer for the assistance of the Holy Spirit, Scripture reading, the sermon, intercessory prayer, Lord's Prayer, Apostles' Creed, another metrical psalm, and finally the Benediction.

The Book of Common Order contained, further, the Psalms, with doxologies, the Confession of Faith used at Geneva, regulations regarding ministers, elders, deacons, superintendents, session-discipline, excommunication, sick-visiting, burial, marriage, baptism, communion, and fasting, with some family prayers, and graces, and prayers for special occasions. Often Calvin's Catechism was bound up with the

Book of Common Order. It was generally used for religious instruction until the Shorter Catechism was adopted in 1648.

Books to read :—

Eustace Percy, 'John Knox.' (1937.)
Henry Cowan, 'John Knox.' (1905.)
John Knox, 'History of the Reformation.'
'Scots Confession, 1560.' (Edited by G. D. Henderson.)

CHAPTER VIII.

REFORMED SCOTLAND.

Mary, Queen of Scots.—Mary, Queen of Scots, returned to Scotland in August 1561. She was only eighteen, and for thirteen years she had lived in France, where for a year and a half she had been Queen. She was now a widow, and in the existing state of things her prospects in France were poor. It seemed best for her to go home to her Scottish kingdom. But the Scottish climate was less kindly, the condition of civilisation was ruder, and court life was scarcely what she had known in Paris and Blois. Popular loyalty welcomed eagerly the beautiful young queen; but she proved unequal to her difficult task. Her father, James V., had died when she was the merest infant. Her mother and she had been so long parted that they can have known one another but slightly. The leading nobles, to whom she might naturally have looked for wise counsel, appear to have been singularly lacking in patriotism and lamentably weak in ideals and character. The times were perplexing. Very soon things began to go wrong. Tragedy followed tragedy—the murder of Rizzio, the murder of Darnley, the strange marriage with Bothwell, the imprisonment at Lochleven, the defeat at Langside. Within seven years it was all over, and the unfortunate queen was a prisoner in an English castle.

Mary was a devout Romanist, and accustomed to regard Protestants with horror and disgust. Had she not been present in the Chateau of Amboise, when only a few months before she left France so many hundreds of them had been massacred in the courtyard, hung from the balconies or drowned in the Loire? Had she not pledged herself to bring back Scotland to the Roman allegiance?

Her presence in Scotland was naturally a very serious cause of alarm for Knox and his associates. One Mass seemed to him more fearful than an invading army. He became extremely excited, had several distressing interviews with the queen, and became her implacable enemy, believing the newly accomplished Reformation in jeopardy. Certainly the organisation of the Church was retarded. Those who opposed it now had strong backing, and those who were unwilling to support it to the extent of sacrifice now had a good excuse.

Nor did the difficulties cease when Mary went into exile and the Protestant Earl of Moray took over the regency for the infant James VI. (born 1566). Moray was a pious Christian and a convinced Protestant, but political considerations inclined him to compromise, while to Knox the times seemed to call for anything but that. After Moray was assassinated (1570) there were troubled years under one regent after another, intrigues by the friends of the hapless Queen Mary, plots to influence the young king, and, in the religious world, the continued serious financial helplessness of the Church, the warning provided by the startling news of the massacre of thousands of Huguenots (French Protestants) in Paris on St Bartholomew's Day, 1572, and the beginning of the attempt of the State for its own ends to force Episcopacy upon the Church in Scotland.

The Death of Knox.—John Knox died on 24th November 1572. He was to the end the life and soul of the Protestant cause which he had done so much to establish in his native land. Although he failed to realise many of his ideals, and was unable to bend the Scottish nobles to his will with regard to Church policy, he retained his power over the people, and especially his authority in the pulpit.

James Melville has left a famous description of him in his last days. He calls him "that most notable prophet and apostle of our nation," and tells how he heard him teach at St Andrews, and took notes of what he said. "In the opening up of his text he was moderate the space of half an hour, but when he entered to application, he made me so grew and tremble that I could not hold a pen to write." "Mr Knox would come in and repose himself in our College yard and call us scholars unto him and bless us and exhort us to know

God and His work in our country and stand by the good cause." "He was very weak. I saw him every day of his doctrine go slowly and warily with a furring of matricks about his neck, a staff in the one hand and good, godly Richard Ballantyne, his servant, holding up the other oxter, from the Abbey to the Parish Kirk, and by the said Richard and another servant lifted up to the pulpit, where he behoved to lean at first entry, but ere he had done with his sermon, he was so active and vigorous that he was like to ding the pulpit in blads and fly out of it."

Knox was buried near St Giles's Church in Edinburgh, and over his grave the Regent Morton uttered the words: "Here lieth a man who in his life never feared the face of man."

Tulchan Bishops.—Even before the death of Knox the Church had at the Leith Convention (1572) found itself obliged to accept a modified form of Episcopacy. Bishops were disliked for a number of reasons. The bishops of the pre-Reformation Church represented a system under which the clergy had absolute control of the means of salvation. The abolition of the tyranny to which this led was one of the purposes of the Reformation. Again, the bishop, when State appointed, was apt to be a mere creature of the monarch, and spiritual freedom was thus endangered. The Presbyterian system was felt to be better, because it gave the layman a true place in the Church and yet did not place the Church under lay control. In 1572 there was no thought of declaring Episcopacy necessary. No divine right of Episcopacy was suggested. Superintendents, however, had proved serviceable from the point of view of discipline. It appeared also that if there were bishops of any sort some at least of the Church's lost wealth would once more become available for it. Bishops, besides, would be able to stand up for the Church's interests with the government, and would be useful intermediaries between Church and State. For such reasons, and under pressure from the Regent Morton, the Church yielded. Knox himself acquiesced in the arrangement.

It was, however, neither one thing nor another. Said one at the time: "There be three kinds of bishops: my Lord Bishop; my Lord's Bishop; and the Lord's Bishop. My Lord Bishop was in the Papistry; my Lord's Bishop is now when my lord gets the fat of the benefice and the Bishop makes his title sure; the Lord's Bishop is the true minister of the Gospel." Others called these new bishops, tulchans. "When a cow will not give her milk, they stuff a calf's skin full of straw and set it down before the cow, and that was called a tulchan. So these bishops, possessing the title and the benefice, without the office, they wist not what name to give them, and so they called them tulchan bishops."

Andrew Melville.—An entirely new situation was created when Andrew Melville appeared upon the scene. He had been born in 1545 and educated at St Andrews University, which he left with the reputation of being "the best philosopher, poet, and Grecian of any young master in the land." Proceeding to the famous University of Paris and afterwards to that of Poitiers, he further extended his learning. He had trying experiences in those days of civil war between Romanists and Huguenots, and found it advisable to leave France and continue his studies at Geneva where the Reformation was well established. Calvin had died in 1564, but Theodore Beza, his successor, was a distinguished scholar, orator, and organiser. One utterance of his will never be forgotten: "Sire, it belongs in truth to the Church of God to endure blows and not to inflict them; but it will also please your majesty to remember that the Church is an anvil that has worn out many hammers."

Melville remained for some years at Geneva as a university teacher, and was in close touch both with the leaders of Reformation thought and with the practical troubles to which the Protestants of France were then subject. In 1574 he returned to Scotland. His library at this time is described as "rich and rare, of the best authors, in all languages, arts, and sciences, clearly declaring by his instruments what a craftsman he was." Beza wrote that the greatest token of affection the Church of Geneva could show to Scotland was that they allowed themselves to be deprived of Melville that thereby the Church of Scotland might be enriched.

First as Principal of Glasgow University and then as Principal of St Mary's College, St Andrews, Melville gave first-rate service to Scottish education, and especially to the production of efficient ministers. The fearlessness and determination of this new leader of the Church were shown in many incidents. When the regent threatened to have him hung or banished, he replied: "Tush, threaten your courtiers in that way. It is all the same to me whether I rot in the air on in the ground. The earth is the Lord's: my fatherland is wherever well-doing is. . . . It will not lie in your power to hang or exile God's truth."

Yet, again, when brought before the King's Council in connection with complaints he had uttered regarding interference with the Church, one of the nobles exclaiming: "Who dare subscribe these treasonable articles?" Andrew Melville stepped forward and took up the pen, declaring: "We dare, and will subscribe and render our lives in the cause."

The Growth of Presbyterianism.—Melville became the centre of hostility to any form of Episcopacy. The main result of his efforts was the Second Book of Discipline, accepted by the Church in 1581. This is a document which remains of importance in connection with the constitution of our Scottish Church. According to Melville the office-bearers of the Church are ministers (pastors or bishops), elders, and deacons. Doctors or teachers he also recognises as required. Ministers should have a sense of vocation, should be elected in accordance with the will of the congregation, and should be ordained by the laying on of hands. "Ordination is the separation and sanctifying of the person appointed by God and His Kirk after he be well tried and found qualified." They have to preach the Word, administer the sacraments, solemnise marriages, care for the spiritual wellbeing of the people, visit the sick. Elders, who are to be annually elected, and who represent the laity in the government of the Church, assist the minister in the spiritual supervision of the parish, and watch over the moral conduct of the congregation. "As the pastors should be diligent in teaching and sowing the Word, so the elders should be careful in seeking the fruits of the same among the people." Deacons have as their special charge the care of the poor.

The government of the Church is in the hands of recognised courts, from General Assembly to Kirk Session. The civil magistrates, that is, King, Parliament, and local authorities, have the duty of assisting and maintaining the Church, protecting it from corruption, and seeing that it is enabled to apply its discipline, providing for the maintenance of ministers, schools, and the poor, making laws for the advancement of religion, but not interfering in matters that are purely spiritual. "The civil power should command the spiritual to exercise and do their office according to the Word of God; the spiritual rulers should require the Christian magistrate to minister justice and punish vice and to maintain the liberty and quietness of the Kirk."

The struggle between parties went on. Archbishop Patrick Adamson of St Andrews was perhaps the best representative of those who favoured Episcopacy, and James VI. was now old enough to take an active interest in the controversy. By the Black Acts of 1584 Parliament gave temporary victory to the Episcopalian party, but finally in 1592 Melville secured what has sometimes been called the Magna Charta of Scottish Presbyterianism, when King and Parliament acknowledged and ratified Church government by General Assemblies, Synods, Presbyteries, and Kirk Sessions, legalising the main principles of the Second Book of Discipline.

The first General Assembly, a small gathering of ministers and laymen, took place in 1560. Since then Assemblies had met, at first twice a year, later once a year, and had proved themselves effective and indeed necessary to the maintenance and development of the Reformed Church. Knox regarded the General Assembly as vital for the preservation of good order and unity in doctrine. The Assembly retained its importance in the Scottish Church. It was a representative body, ministers, nobles, burgesses, and university teachers sharing in its activities, and the mind and will of the Scottish people being here more plainly to be discerned than in Parliament or anywhere else.

Synods were half-yearly meetings of ministers and representative elders which, under the General Assembly, dealt with Church affairs in large districts, roughly corresponding to the medieval dioceses. In many respects they had the responsibilities of the former bishops.

Presbyteries were a new development. There was no mention of them in the First Book of Discipline, but they began to be organised about 1580. Their institution was encouraged by the proved usefulness of such bodies in France. The Synod was sub-divided into Presbyteries. These consisted of the ministers of all the churches within a restricted area, with one elder from each congregation. The Scottish Presbyteries had a double origin. There had from the Reformation been a system of regular meetings of ministers and elders for Scripture study. These were called Exercises. They formed the nucleus of the new Presbyteries, and these long continued to begin their meetings with a sermon and discussion which they called the Exercise. On the other hand, Synods had tended to be overburdened as the number of ministers and organised parishes increased, and it was really necessary to have part of the work delegated to more local bodies. The duties of a Presbytery came to be similar to those of a Synod, but on a smaller scale. The Presbytery was thus a natural outcome of the practical requirements of an increasingly active and efficient Church. It is the Presbytery that is responsible for the ordination and discipline of ministers.

The fourth of these characteristic Presbyterian Church courts was the Kirk Session, which was in charge of the spiritual affairs of a single parish, and consisted of the minister and the elders and deacons. This graded system of courts—Assembly, Synod, Presbytery, and Kirk Session—is regarded as one of the outstanding features of a fully organised Presbyterian Church.

It naturally took a long time thus to rebuild the Church and set it in order. In the early days of the Reformation there were comparatively few men sufficiently trained to undertake the important work of preaching, and most of the parishes had for a time to be content with a semi-qualified 'reader' who read to the assembled congregation a service from the Book of Common Order.

Progress in the matter of Education was also very slow; but schools were peculiarly important in the interests of reform, for people must be taught to read and to use their minds if they were to know the Bible and to be able to take an intelligent part in the public worship of the Church and in its government.

In all its efforts in this and other directions the Church was seriously hampered by want of money. Before the Reformation the Church had been too rich; but most of its wealth had now been appropriated by the Crown or the nobles or local authorities, and the Church was certainly left too poor to be efficient.

On the other hand, the degraded condition into which religion had fallen before the Reformation had made the country very hearty in its reception of the new state of affairs; and the Reformation in Scotland was not only most thorough in its character, but most widespread in the extent of its acceptance. Romanism almost completely disappeared, and for the nation as a whole, religion, from having been a form and a superstition, became a reality and an inspiration.

Books to read :—

W. Morison, 'Andrew Melville.' (Famous Scots Series.)
J. Moffatt, 'The Presbyterian Churches.' (1928.)
W. MacMillan, 'The Worship of the Scottish Reformed Church, 1550-1638.' (1930.)

CHAPTER IX.

THE EARLY SEVENTEENTH CENTURY.

King James and the Church.—Religion took a chief place in the life of the seventeenth century. In Scotland, king, parliament, and town councils, as well as all classes of the people, were concerned about religious affairs. Even those who were furthest from a Christian way of living assumed the truth of Christianity and the value of Bible standards, and submitted to Church oversight.

The proper relation between Church and State occupied much attention. In England the State had taken a lead in the Reformation, and Henry VIII. had assumed the headship of the Church in place of the Pope. Thereafter the government continued to direct the country's religious life, and we have the arrangement (which is generally called Erastian) under which the Church is more or less a department of the State, like the Post Office or Board of Education. This was the kind of scheme that approved itself to James VI., and he said so very plainly in his book, 'Basilikon Doron,' which was published in 1598. The control of Church affairs James regarded as "no small point of his office."

Quite a different view was that of Andrew Melville. He is sometimes thought to have gone at times too far in the other direction, and to have been inclined to make light of the function of the State, and to assign to the Church a place of very decided priority. David Black and other ministers were apt to be unduly arrogant and to overdo freedom of speech, even towards the king. James called such men "fanatic spirits," and heartily disliked them. Certainly if such a view is pressed to an extreme, it comes to be very like that of the Middle Ages Pope Hildebrand, who wanted the Church to rule the world. This reminds us of some parts of the Old Testament, and is government by Theocracy. There was a certain approach to this in Scotland when the Covenanters were triumphant; but even with them it was never, as with Hildebrand, government by clergy, but always by clerical and lay representatives together.

Andrew Melville's general position was that there are two independent departments—the spiritual and the civil—the Church being responsible for the one and the State for the other, and neither deriving its authority from the other, but each direct from God. He said somewhat brusquely to James VI.: "There are two kings and two kingdoms in Scotland: there is King James, the head of this commonwealth, and there is Christ Jesus, the King of the Church, whose subject King James the Sixth is, and of whose kingdom he is not a king, nor a lord, nor a head, but a member." Melville seemed to James to be a dangerous democrat. "No bishop, no king," he prophesied. And from such teaching he turned naturally to Episcopacy, under which through the bishops he was able to control the Church, as had been done in England.

By very careful and cautious steps he encouraged the acceptance of bishops in Scotland, and he seemed likely to succeed in establishing this system without serious opposition. As long as it was not suggested that bishops were necessary to the existence of a true Church, many people were quite ready to agree that they were useful, and might on this ground be permitted. And under James the bishops did indeed confine themselves to the kind of work that had been done by Knox's superintendents. James was not interested in any special theory of the nature of the Church. What he wished was that the authority should ultimately be in his hands. "The bishops," he said, "must rule the ministers, and the king rule both."

Some people were very much afraid that James's plan was only a beginning, and that after he had introduced Episcopacy in this extremely mild form a very different form would not be long in following, and before the country saw what was happening Rome would once again have the upper hand. The keenest Presbyterians therefore tried to hold an Assembly at Aberdeen in 1605 in spite of King James, but he dealt most sternly with the attempt, and as a result Andrew Melville, his nephew James Melville, John Forbes of Alford, and other leaders of this party suffered exile, and were no longer in a position to interfere with his wishes. By 1610 he had a fully organised Episcopalian system in Scotland.

But the king was not content with this success. After he inherited the throne of England on the death of Queen Elizabeth in 1603 he quite sensibly did all he could to make his two kingdoms one in fact as well as in name ; and naturally he desired to have the same religious practices observed in both. He had decided in favour of Episcopacy, and now he began to bring Scottish Church worship into line with what he found in England. The services there were much liker those of the pre-Reformation Church than were those of Reformed France, Holland, Switzerland, and Scotland.

The Fear of Rome.—In 1618 James insisted upon the Scottish Church accepting the Five Articles of Perth : kneeling at Communion, permission to have Communion privately, permission of private Baptism, Confirmation by bishops, and the observance of Christmas, Easter, and other similar Church occasions. Strong opposition developed ; and amongst those who were most hostile was Alexander Henderson, minister at Leuchars in Fife, who later became the leader of the Covenanting party. He and others objected on two grounds to what James was doing. They thought that the king should leave all such matters to the free decision of the General Assembly, and they thought that the changes, though small in themselves, were in the direction of Rome. Kneeling at Communion in particular appeared to them too suggestive of Transubstantiation.

Everybody was terribly afraid of Rome in those days. They did not think of Romanism just as an inferior kind of Christianity. They did not believe that it was Christianity at all. They were convinced that with great cunning the devil had managed to persuade the Church in pre-Reformation days to desert right ways of worship and of thinking, and to follow wrong ways which made them really, though unconsciously, his servants. The Pope was therefore the Antichrist of the Book of Revelation, and Romanism was an anti-God movement. The devil was very strong and very clever, and the Reformed Church had to be most careful that he did not manage somehow to trick them away from the purity of the old Christian faith to which at the Reformation they had returned. Therefore they were most suspicious of anything that reminded them at all of Romish customs. They wanted to keep as far away from these as possible, and in their terror they were apt to avoid not only corruptions and abuses that had crept into the Church, but also other practices that were extremely ancient and quite harmless or even helpful.

The power of Rome was being made very clear at this time. The Thirty Years' War on the Continent began in 1618, and was in its early stages a desperate struggle between Protestantism and Romanism. A great Reformed conference or synod which met at Dort in Holland in 1618 was so worried about Romanism that it thought it wise not to allow the slightest departure from the ways laid down by Calvin. In 1620 the Protestants in Bohemia, whose queen was a daughter of James VI., suffered a crushing defeat at the hands of the Romanist Hapsburgs. At this time many Scots served abroad with Gustavus Adolphus of Sweden and other Protestant leaders, and they brought home vivid stories. No wonder there was fear of Rome and of Romish ways.

Feeling in Scotland grew stronger in favour of freedom for the Church to guide its own spiritual life, puritan simplicity of worship to avoid Romish superstition and to make sure of inward reality in approaching God, and the Presbyterian form of Church government to keep things out of the power of the State and give the people a share in the regulation of religious affairs.

King Charles and the Church.—In 1625 Charles I. succeeded to his father's throne and his father's religious policy. The new king was a man of principle and piety, but though he had high ideals he had not his father's skill in the matter of getting his own way, and he soon unhappily created an atmosphere of suspicion. Some schemes of his in connection with finance caused irritation amongst the Scottish nobles and landed proprietors, and roused them against his view that he was an absolute monarch who might do whatever he thought best. It was not very long before ministers and people found that he meant to be an absolute monarch with regard to religion also. Charles was advised in Church affairs by Laud, whom he made Archbishop of

Canterbury ; but even the visit which these leaders of Church and State paid to Scotland in 1633 did not give them an understanding of the general feelings. Their methods gave rise to very grave dissatisfaction.

In order to bring the Church of Scotland into line with that of England a Book of Canons was issued in 1636, containing many rules which were at variance with Scottish Reformed practice. This was followed by the Prayer Book of 1637 which was ordered to be used in all parish churches. It was like the English Prayer Book, and Scottish people feared to have "our poor country made an English Province." It had been carefully revised by Charles and Laud, and two of the Scottish bishops had helped with it ; but the Scottish ministers had not been officially consulted, and it was not submitted to any court of the Church. It was imposed on the Church by the king's authority in direct contradiction to the doctrine of Spiritual Independence, and in accordance with Charles's ideas as to his duty under the doctrine of the Divine Right of Kings. And besides hostility to the methods employed there was serious alarm at some of the contents of the book, which seemed to have a Romish character, and certainly restored much which Scotland had been at some pains to reject at the Reformation.

The Scots did not object to a prayer book being read in church. They had long been accustomed to Knox's liturgy. But they objected very much to what they thought was happening at this time. Matters came to a head on 23rd July 1637 when in St Giles's Church in Edinburgh Jenny Geddes threw her stool at the clergyman who first attempted to read the new service book. "Dost thou say mass at my lug," she is said to have exclaimed. A riot followed, and both the Church leaders and the nobles felt that the time was ripe for putting an end to the king's attempts at absolute rule. There was a great deal of correspondence with London, and much excitement in various parts of Scotland, and early in 1638 the supporters of the cause of freedom were summoned to Edinburgh and the National Covenant was produced for signature.

The National Covenant.—The idea of a Covenant was not new. Both in Scotland and abroad men had frequently bound themselves solemnly together to support some cause, political or religious. Covenants are repeatedly mentioned in the Bible, and this fact added peculiar sacredness to the occasion.

The National Covenant was drawn up by Alexander Henderson and Archibald Johnston of Wariston. Henderson was the most balanced of the Covenant leaders. "A more modest, humble spirit of so great parts and deserved authority with all the greatest of the Isles lives not this day in the Reformed Churches," it was said. He was generally reckoned "by much the wisest and gravest of the Scots." Johnston was a rising young lawyer, a religious enthusiast of the extreme Puritan type, and an ardent supporter of Presbyterianism.

The Covenant consisted of three parts. It began by repeating the Negative Confession, a very strongly worded rejection of all Roman error which had been issued under James VI. in 1581, and which all persons in office had been required to sign. The second part was a list of the numerous Acts which the Scottish Parliament at one time or another had passed against Romanism. And finally there was a short section proclaiming the intention of the Covenanters, "to recover the purity and liberty of the Gospel," and their prayer "that religion and righteousness may flourish in the land to the Glory of God, the honour of our king, and peace and comfort of us all." The document as a whole was such that little objection could be taken to it, and from the point of view of its promoters it was a great success.

The signing of the Covenant was begun in the Greyfriars Kirk in Edinburgh on 28th February 1638. There were remarkable scenes of religious and patriotic excitement. Nobles, gentry, ministers, and burgesses enthusiastically took the Covenant. Copies of the document speedily appeared all over the country, and the acceptance of the Covenant by individuals and congregations was a solemn dedication ceremony. Some subscribed their names with their blood. Seldom have Scots been so united, so fired with zeal, so exalted in spirit, so resolute to obey God rather than men. The Covenanting party carried all before it, and soon practically controlled the government of the country.

There was opposition from some who were unwilling to desert the king, or who were believers in Episcopacy, but it was timid and futile. The most celebrated of those who stood out against the Covenant were the six Aberdeen Doctors. They were by no means in favour of Rome, nor were they followers of Laud, but they thought it a mistake to be so intolerant of bishops and ceremonies, and regarded these as, not perhaps essential, but certainly allowable, and useful for discipline and as evidence of unity with other branches of the universal Church.

King Charles took the Scottish outburst very seriously, declaring that as long as the Covenant was in force his authority in Scotland was practically nothing, a position which he would rather die than accept. He was obliged, however, to agree to a General Assembly to meet in Glasgow in November 1638. At this celebrated Assembly, which gathered in the ancient Cathedral, the laity were strongly in evidence. Alexander Henderson was Moderator and Archibald Johnston was Clerk. The Marquis of Hamilton represented the king, but when it became evident that he could not in the least control the course of events, he declared the Assembly dissolved. In spite of this the Assembly continued in session, overthrew the Episcopal system, rejected the recent innovations in worship, and reasserted the place of elders in the courts of the Church. Feeling having become extremely bitter, and charity in consequence almost forgotten, the Assembly even went the length of excommunicating some of the chief opponents of the Covenant.

The Episcopalian experiment had thus completely failed, and the result of the efforts of James VI. and Charles I. was simply to strengthen Scottish adherence to spiritual freedom, Protestantism and Presbyterianism.

Books to read :—

W. L. Mathieson, 'Politics and Religion in Scotland.' (1902.)
R. L. Orr, 'Alexander Henderson.' (1919.)
S. Rutherfurd, 'Letters.' (Bonar's edition.)
R. Baillie, 'Letters and Journals.' (Bannatyne Club edition.)

CHAPTER X.

COVENANTERS TRIUMPHANT.

The Solemn League and Covenant.—"We have now cast down the walls of Jericho." These words, which were meant to sum up the achievements of the Glasgow Assembly of 1638, have been attributed to Alexander Henderson, the Moderator. Episcopacy was overthrown, and Puritanism remained in power from that date until the Restoration in 1660.

Puritanism was the result of Calvin's doctrine of the Sovereignty of God. From this it was concluded that the worshipper must worship directly in sincerity and simplicity, and not let ceremonies or ornaments or anything else come between him and God. It was felt that supposed aids tended to become ends instead of means, and so thwarted rather than helped devotion, and amounted to idolatry. It was also concluded that true faith must show itself in a life of obedience to the will of God ; and the Puritans were therefore very strict in morals, in Sunday observance, and in attention to what was laid down in the Bible. Their enemies thought them too scrupulous and precise and serious, and there was certainly the danger of their becoming self-righteous and pharisaic. They tended to make a ritual of no ritual, and to lay too much stress upon outward acts and too little upon motive.

King Charles attempted to crush the Covenanting Party by force, but a strong Scottish army was raised, with the words "For Christ's Crown and Covenant" in gold letters upon its banner, and under the experienced General Leslie, was able to prevent any interference with the newly won liberties. Presently (1642) the king found himself at war with the more democratic section of his subjects in England. A deputation from the English Parliamentary party visited Edinburgh in 1643, and the Solemn League and Covenant was drawn up and signed. It was a treaty between the Presbyterian leaders, who now controlled Scotland, and those in England who had been driven into revolt by King Charles's determination to rule as an absolute monarch. The Covenanters in Scotland and the Parliament in England made common cause against tyranny.

The Solemn League and Covenant is not to be confused with the National Covenant of 1638. The new document aimed at securing the freedom of the Church of Scotland, and making the Churches of the three kingdoms as like one another as possible in doctrine, worship, and government on Presbyterian lines, Episcopacy being condemned and the rights and privileges of Parliaments asserted, and the enemies of the Solemn League threatened with " condign punishment."

One result was the despatch of a Scottish army to fight in England on the Parliamentary side. It took part in various important engagements up to the conclusive battle of Naseby. In 1646 King Charles surrendered to the Scots, but next year they handed him over to the English army, who were responsible for his execution in 1649.

The Westminster Assembly.—Another result was the appointment of a few Scottish ministers and elders to take part in the Westminster Assembly, which began its sittings in July 1643 and remained in session till February 1648. It had been designed " for the settling of the government and liturgy of the Church of England and for vindicating and clearing of the doctrine of the said Church from false aspersions and interpretations." England did not in the end accept Presbyterianism as the Scots had fondly hoped, but Scotland was permanently affected, for it received as its standards of doctrine, worship, and government the principal documents issued by this Assembly, including Westminster Confession, Larger Catechism, Shorter Catechism, Directory for the Public Worship of God, Form of Presbyterial Church Government, and a new version of the Metrical Psalms. These were all largely the work of English Puritans. The Scots took care that nothing was approved that was contrary to what they had been accustomed to in Scotland, but there can be no doubt that in this period English Puritanism considerably influenced the Scottish Church.

The Westminster Confession of Faith (1647) deals with the Church's beliefs. The teaching is Calvinistic. It puts Scripture in the forefront, and proceeds to speak of God, the Trinity, Predestination and Election, the Fall of Man, Justification, Saving Faith, Repentance unto Life, the Civil Magistrate, the Church, the Sacraments, and other matters of doctrine. The document is long, and goes very minutely into many difficult theological problems. It took the place of the Scots Confession, and it remains to this day the "chief subordinate standard" of our Church.

The Shorter Catechism (1648) is a most excellent brief statement of doctrine, beginning with the question, "What is the chief end of Man?" with its famous answer, "Man's chief end is to glorify God and to enjoy Him for ever," and, in its 107 questions and answers, giving a summary which, until recently, was imprinted upon the memory of every Scottish child.

The Directory for the Public Worship of God (1645), which replaced the Book of Common Order, was not a liturgy in any strict sense, but a very common-sense guide to the conduct of religious services. The Order of Service which it recommends begins with a Call to Worship, followed by a short Prayer; a metrical psalm; reading from the Bible; a long Prayer, including Confession, Supplication, and Intercession; the Sermon; a Prayer of Thanksgiving, followed by the Lord's Prayer; another psalm; and the Benediction. Careful directions are given as to the orderly celebration of the Sacraments of Baptism and the Lord's Supper; and instruction is given as to the observance of Sunday, marriage services, visitation of the sick, and the burial of the dead.

The Westminster documents have exerted great influence in Scotland and in every country where Scots have settled.

The Scots who took part in the Assembly were Alexander Henderson, Robert Baillie, Samuel Rutherfurd, George Gillespie, Johnston of Wariston, and Lord Maitland (afterwards Duke of Lauderdale). Baillie was Principal of Glasgow University, and his observant 'Letters and Journals' are invaluable for their interesting information about the period. Rutherfurd is best known for his devout and imaginative

'Letters,' mostly written while he was exiled in Aberdeen on account of his hostility to Episcopacy, and for his 'Lex Rex,' which is an important work in political science. George Gillespie, though a very young man, was a first-rate debater and a most ardent Presbyterian. Maitland was later to change his opinions, and to govern Scotland in the interest of King Charles II. The others we already know.

Divided Opinions.—The Solemn League and Covenant was ordered to be signed everywhere throughout Scotland, and was used as a test of loyalty to those in authority. One finds Kirk Sessions seeking out such as had not subscribed. Some, like Dr John Forbes of Corse, the best known of the Aberdeen Doctors, thought it wise to go abroad in order to escape danger.

Those who disapproved of the Solemn League and Covenant found a brilliant champion in the Marquis of Montrose. He had been at first on the Covenanting side, but had developed a distaste for the more extreme Presbyterians including Argyll, the outstanding nobleman of the party, and he could not accept an alliance with English rebels. His personal gallantry and the startling dash of his campaigns made him a glamorous figure, but he gained little support for the royal cause, and was at last disastrously defeated at Philiphaugh in September 1645. As a result of a later outbreak after the death of Charles I. he was captured and cruelly hanged in 1650.

Difference of opinion was now creeping in among the Presbyterians, and soon we find two distinct parties: on the one hand, the Protesters, the strict type devoted to the Covenants, who would only support the king if the king would support them; and on the other hand, the Resolutioners, who were broader in their outlook and who were prepared to give and take, anxious to preserve the monarchy and hopeful that things would yet work out satisfactorily for the Church on moderate lines. The former would have none in public office but strict Covenanters. The latter were involved in the Engagement of 1648, a compromise arrangement with Charles I., which led to an ill-fated expedition into England under Hamilton. The failure of this effort at Preston left Scotland in the power of the sterner party, who by the Act of Classes of 1649 cleansed the army and all public life of everyone but their own sympathisers.

Cromwell in Scotland.—The Scots were horrified when Charles I. was put to death in January 1649; they at once proclaimed Charles II. to be king, and when he had been persuaded to sign the Covenants he was crowned at Scone in 1650. Oliver Cromwell was now in control of English affairs and he immediately invaded Scotland, defeating the army of the Protesters at Dunbar (1650), and finishing the war by his victory over Charles II. at Worcester (1651), afterwards treating Scotland as a conquered land and absorbing it into his new commonwealth. In religion he was an Independent, and he found himself more in sympathy with the Protesters than with the Resolutioners. The General Assembly proved a hindrance to the Dictator, and he had it disbanded in 1653.

Cromwell's military tyranny was not long in becoming distasteful to the Scottish people, and their preference for monarchy was confirmed. At the same time the narrow, rigid, gloomy, and intolerant attitude of the leading Protesters caused a reaction in favour of a more moderate religious policy, and it is not surprising that the Resolutioners in 1660 welcomed the Restoration, even though it proved to carry with it the return of Episcopacy.

Kirkton gives a glowing account of the spiritual condition of Scotland in the strict Puritan period: "I verily believe there were more souls converted to Christ in that short period of time than in any since the Reformation; nor was there ever greater purity and plenty of the means of grace than was in their time. Ministers were painful, people were diligent. . . . So truly religion was at that time in very good case and the Lord present in Scotland." But Patrick Gillespie, James Guthrie, Johnston of Wariston, and Samuel Rutherfurd, the outstanding figures of this type, were responsible for an oppressive spiritual tyranny, from which Episcopacy presently offered escape. Prominent among the Resolutioners were Robert Douglas, a minister endowed with sagacity and prudence, as well as of distinguished appearance, and David Dickson, in his early days a most moving preacher of the Gospel, and later, as a professor, the author of many helpful commentaries on the Bible.

Episcopacy Again.—Charles II. when restored to his throne showed no desire to associate again with those who had supported him at the price of subscribing the Covenants. Guthrie and Johnston were executed, as was also Argyll. Episcopacy was restored and bishops were selected. James Sharp, who had been one of the leading Resolutioners, was created Archbishop of St Andrews, an appointment which made him an object of special hatred to his former Presbyterian associates, who regarded him as a traitor.

The most admirable of the new bishops was undoubtedly Robert Leighton, a saintly man, little interested in the great controversy of the times between Presbyterianism and Episcopacy and Independency, condemning "furious zeals and endless debates," but much interested in the Bible and in living as in the presence of God. One of his favourite books was Thomas à Kempis's 'Imitation of Christ.' He was Bishop of Dunblane and acted for a time as Archbishop of Glasgow. His 'Accommodation' was a scheme for reconciling Episcopacy and Presbyterianism. "They do much better together," he said, "than either of them does apart." But his compromise attracted neither party. In 1674 he retired in disappointment to private life in England.

It was a moderate form of Episcopacy that prevailed in Scotland from 1661 to 1690. No one thought of introducing what would have pleased Laud. The archbishops and bishops had the controlling voice, in close relation with the civil representatives of the king. Synods, Presbyteries, and Kirk Sessions, however, continued as under Presbyterianism. Discipline was somewhat relaxed, but the former careful observance of Sunday persisted, and much anxious attention was given to Popery and Quakerism, witchcraft and charming. Doctrine became rather less rigid, but the Westminster Confession and Shorter Catechism remained the popular standards. In worship, the metrical psalms and extemporary prayer were used just as by the Presbyterians. Surplices were not worn, and bishops did not confirm. No liturgy was employed at the Sunday services, and the sermon retained its old place of supremacy. Only the regular use of the Creed, the Lord's Prayer, and the Doxology distinguished the new form of worship from the old. This moderation made Episcopacy easy for the people to accept, but also easy by-and-by to abandon. The half-heartedness of the system did not make it attractive. Further, the leaders of the Episcopalian party were not on the whole very distinguished or effective, and did not manage to win the heart or capture the imagination of Scotland.

Episcopacy also suffered from association with bad government. Charles II. took little personal interest in Scottish affairs, but those who acted for him—Middleton, Lauderdale, Rothes, and their subordinates—were in only too many cases deficient in sense and in character. They dealt most unwisely with the Covenanters, persecuting them in a way that only made them more obstinate and extreme, and that gained for them public sympathy. And, in addition, fear of Rome was revived by the knowledge that the king's heir was a Romanist, and by the dreadful treatment of the French Huguenots by Louis XIV. before and after the Revocation of the Edict of Nantes in 1685. Episcopacy was still popularly suspected of being the road to Rome. It was thus almost inevitable that the pendulum should swing again, Episcopacy pass into disfavour, and Presbyterianism be established more securely than ever, as indeed happened at the Revolution Settlement in 1690.

Books to read :—

'Confession of Faith, &c.' (Blackwood's edition.)
W. Beveridge, 'A Short History of the Westminster Assembly.' (1904.)
J. Buchan, 'Montrose.' (1928.)
E. A. Knox, 'Robert Leighton.' (1930.)

CHAPTER XI.

THE COVENANTERS UNDER PERSECUTION.

Episcopacy in the Ascendant.—The name of the Covenanters is familiar to every Scot and to all in other countries who are interested in religious freedom. The Covenanters were those who subscribed first the National Covenant of 1638 and then the Solemn League and Covenant of 1643, and who regarded these as symbols of devotion to true religion. We have already studied the early history of those staunch upholders of Presbyterianism. Their triumph over royal tyranny and over Episcopacy was succeeded by a period when religious leaders ruled in Scotland almost as in Old Testament story. Latterly their own extremeness contributed to the ease with which Episcopacy was restored by the Rescissory Act (1661) and other measures of Charles II.

Presbyterianism was cast down, but not destroyed. By an Act of 1662 all ministers who were not prepared to accept Episcopacy and to seek recognition by patron and bishop had to give up their parishes. Rather to the surprise of the government some three hundred did so. It was, of course, extremely difficult to find substitutes for so many, and the new Episcopalian 'curates' were not of the quality of the men whom they replaced. Gilbert Burnet, a well-known Episcopalian historian, says "they were the worst preachers I ever heard; they were ignorant to a reproach, and many of them were openly vicious. They were a disgrace to orders and the sacred functions; and were indeed the dregs and refuse of the northern parts." Another writer declared that there were complaints in the north that farmers could not get lads to herd their cows, for all had gone to be Episcopalian 'curates.' There has been some exaggeration with regard to the unfitness of these new clergy. They had all qualified for the ministry in the ordinary way; but they had not hitherto been found suitable for any parish. Even had they been exemplary in every respect they would have had difficulty in ousting the deprived ministers from their place in the hearts of those people amongst whom they had devoutly lived and devotedly laboured. The great majority of the 'outed' Presbyterian ministers were from the South-West of Scotland. This became the main centre of Covenanting activity. There were likewise Covenanters in many other parts of the country; and though many were of the poorer classes they included also noblemen and lairds and merchants. In the North-East of Scotland, however, the feeling was different. Episcopacy had been well represented by such men as Bishop Patrick Forbes, and the political influence of the Huntly family had been in the same direction, so that the Covenants were never in favour.

The Bishops' Dragnet (1663) is the name given to an Act requiring all to attend the services conducted by the Episcopalians. The Scots Mile Act (1663) compelled 'outed' ministers to depart from the districts in which they had served. In 1669 the Assertory Act claimed that the king was supreme in ecclesiastical as well as in civil affairs. The Conventicle Act (1670) was designed to put down the gatherings which resulted from the disinclination of the people to 'hear the curates,' and their desire still to have the ministrations of their former Presbyterian ministers. Conventicles were sometimes merely small assemblies in remote farm-houses or in secluded glens or among the moorland heather. But certain ministers became famous as field preachers, and great crowds secretly assembled to listen to them. John Blackadder (died 1685), minister of Troqueer, had many exciting adventures and narrow escapes as he journeyed on his pony from place to place to preach and celebrate the Sacraments for eager congregations. John Welsh, minister of Irongray (died 1681), a great-grandson of John Knox, was likewise extremely popular as a field preacher.

From Blackadder we have an account of a conventicle in the South-East. The place of meeting was a beautiful spot close to the River Whiteadder, a level haugh well shaded and surrounded by slopes, which provided ample accommodation.

The conventicle occupied three days with preparation, communion, and thanksgiving, the worshippers being lodged at night in neighbouring villages. They were protected on the way to the meeting-place by bands of well-armed horsemen, and the whole occasion passed without interruption from Government troops. Five ministers took part. Tokens were distributed in the regular way on Saturday. Next day the tables were erected on the grass, two long tables parallel to one another and a short one at the one end for the minister and the elements. About two hundred sat down at once, and the tables were served sixteen times, so that some three thousand must have communicated. The action sermon was preached by Welsh, who also served the first two tables, after which the other ministers, including Blackadder, served in turn. Welsh gave the concluding exhortation and pronounced the Benediction.

Persecution.—Everything possible was done to force the people to give up their Presbyterianism. The government employed troopers to search out obstinate Covenanters. In November 1666 several Galloway men came into conflict with some soldiers who had arrested a person for refusing to hear the curate, and one of them loaded a pistol with some pieces of tobacco pipe and wounded a corporal. They then gathered their friends, and riding into Dumfries captured Sir James Turner, who was in command of the troops in the district. They marched north to Ayr and thence to Lanark, their numbers increasing to over a thousand. By the time they reached the outskirts of Edinburgh they were not in such good heart. The country was not rising to support them, and many were practically unarmed and few had any acquaintance with warfare. They were attacked and easily defeated by the dragoons of Sir Thomas Dalziel at Rullion Green on the Pentland slopes.

This accidental outburst on the part of the persecuted startled those in authority, who took it for organised rebellion, and, realising that people were being driven desperate, they tried gentler methods for a time. The Covenanters used to refer to this period when things were a little more bearable as the 'blink.' Indulgences in 1669 and 1672 allowed a few of the outed ministers to be appointed to parishes under certain restrictions. But the stricter Covenanters disdained such approaches, and continued to stay away from church and to attend conventicles instead. Because of the danger of attack, they often appeared in arms on such occasions, and the government was thus led to suspect their meetings to be seditious and rebellious political gatherings rather than religious assemblies. "Let 'em talk what they will," said one; "he who hates a bishop can never love a king." Those who were opposed to the Covenanters excused the persecution as merely punishment for breaking the law, and, in the worst cases, for treason.

Most of the Covenanters, however, were peaceable religious-minded folk, bewildered and maddened by the senseless methods of those at the head of affairs. All who remained Presbyterians were treated as rebels. Sir Walter Scott, who in his 'Old Mortality' shows himself very critical of the Covenanters, admits in his 'Tales of a Grandfather' that it was "as if Satan himself had suggested means of oppression." A host of Highlanders sent to keep order in the South-West worried the Covenanters by their pillaging; dragoons quartered in their houses made home impossible; they were ruined by huge fines; many suffered imprisonment.

In 1679 Archbishop Sharp was savagely murdered on Magus Moor, near St Andrews, by some Presbyterian fanatics. A few weeks later Graham of Claverhouse, attempting to break up an armed conventicle at Drumclog, was repulsed with heavy losses. The victorious Covenanters marched on Glasgow, and soon, with a considerable army of supporters, were encamped close to the bridge over the Clyde at Bothwell. Here, however, they disagreed among themselves, the sterner and the more moderate taking different views as to policy; and when Monmouth with the royal troops came upon them, they were without plan or trusted leaders, and were simply slaughtered. It was a complete defeat. Hundreds of prisoners were marched to Edinburgh and penned into Greyfriars Kirkyard. Some 250 were put on board ship to be sold as slaves on the plantations of America, but the ship was wrecked in the Orkneys and they were drowned.

Heroic Covenanters.—In June 1680 Richard Cameron was responsible for an incident at Sanquhar. He was a preacher who had been ordained in Holland, where numbers of Covenanters were living in exile. In the market-place of this small Dumfriesshire town he caused a proclamation to be posted, disowning Charles II. as a tyrant, declaring war against him as an enemy of the Covenants, and asserting that he would do to his opponents "as they have done to us." Not long afterwards he and his small troop of followers were attacked on Ayres Moss by a company of dragoons, and Cameron was killed. Although he had little education, Cameron seems to have possessed great natural gifts as a preacher. His conviction and earnestness and passion made a tremendous impression upon his audiences, and it was after him that the extremer Covenanters, the Society people, or Hillmen as they were sometimes called, were named the Cameronians.

Donald Cargill had been evicted from his place as minister of the Barony Church of Glasgow, and had for years lived the wandering life of a field preacher. In September 1680 at the Torwood near Falkirk he excommunicated the king, his brother James, Duke of York, Lauderdale, and other principal enemies of the Covenant. There was a price upon his head, and at last he was captured, and was executed in Edinburgh in July 1681.

Alexander Peden was one of the few outstanding Covenanters to escape martyrdom. He had been minister in Glenluce, and after being ejected for his Presbyterianism wandered in Scotland and Ireland, preaching 'weighty and convincing' sermons, suffered several years' imprisonment on the Bass Rock, was put on board ship to be transported to slavery in America, but fortunately liberated at London, lived for a time in a cave near his birthplace in Ayrshire, and died in his old home in 1686. He gained special reputation as a prophet and visionary.

The Test Act of 1681 required all in public office of any kind to renounce the Covenants, and it was succeeded by other measures, which made things still worse for the Presbyterians who held out. In 1685, when Charles II. died, and James II., a convinced Romanist, came to the throne, the persecution was at its very height. Death became the penalty for even attending a field conventicle. This period is remembered as 'the killing time.'

Margaret M'Lachlan and Margaret Wilson were tied to stakes and drowned in the Solway; John Brown of Priesthill, the 'Christian Carrier,' was brutally shot before the eyes of his wife; and every effort was made to wipe out the irreconcilables. A feeble effort at rebellion against James II. was made by Argyll. He came across from Holland to the west coast of Scotland; but his expedition completely failed, and he was seized and executed. This was a political episode not directly connected with the religious situation; but incidentally it led to the drafting of Covenanters from various prisons to Dunnottar Castle near Stonehaven. There in the vaults, where they were huddled together, they were most barbarously treated. One of the Covenanters, looking back upon the persecutions which he had witnessed, sums them up in a gruesome catalogue:—

"His cruelty over the bodies of Christians in chasing and killing upon the fields, many without sentence, and bloody butchering, hanging, heading, dismembering alive, quartering upon scaffolds, imprisoning, laying in irons, torturing by boots, thumbkins, fire-matches, cutting pieces out of the ears of others, banishing and selling as slaves old and young men and women in great numbers, oppressing many others in their estates, forfeiting, robbing, spoiling, pillaging their goods, casting them out of their habitations, interdicting any to reset them, under the pain of being treated after the same manner."

The remnant of the Covenanters were now led by James Renwick. He had been trained in Holland, and returned to Scotland in 1683. "I think," he said, "that if the Lord could be tied to any place, it is to the moors and mosses in Scotland." For several years he was a field preacher, moving about the country tirelessly and always at the risk of his life. He had many hair-breadth escapes from the troopers, but at last was caught in Edinburgh. "What!" said the captain of the guard, "is this boy that Mr Renwick whom the nation has been so troubled with?" He was put to death, the last of the martyrs, on 17th February 1688.

The Turn of the Tide.—The number of the irreconcilable Covenanters in the reign of James II. was not very great, but popular opinion was coming slowly round towards their point of view. Disappointment with what the Episcopalian Church had been able to provide in the way of spiritual nourishment, disgust at the mismanagement of the government and sympathy for the sufferers, made many people wish for a change. James II., in order to obtain liberty of worship for his Romanist friends, was obliged to favour toleration, and in 1687 a new 'Indulgence' allowed 'moderate Presbyterians' to have churches and hold services. Many of the outed ministers took advantage of this opportunity. Quite a number returned from exile in Holland. Meeting-houses were erected for such ministers, and congregations quickly gathered round them. Presbyteries, separate from those of the established Episcopalian Church, were formed, and there were also Synods of ministers and elders, and general meetings (like General Assemblies) began to be held in Edinburgh once a year. Thus there was the framework of a complete new Presbyterian Church ready for the Revolution Settlement.

The North-East was not influenced by this movement, and even after the Revolution Presbyterianism only very slowly regained its hold upon the people there. It must be mentioned also that the extreme Covenanters would have nothing to do with the 'Indulgence,' chiefly because it came from an uncovenanted king, from a Romanist, and from a civil authority. They resolved "to keep their meetings as in former times in the open fields."

King James II. set about putting government in both Scotland and England into the hands of Romanists, and it was not long before the whole country was seething with discontent. James found his position impossible. The English Protestants encouraged William of Orange to come over as their champion and take the throne, and when he landed James fled abroad. There was a good deal of rioting in Scotland, public opinion showing itself strongly against Romanism. In many parishes the people took the opportunity of driving out, sometimes in circumstances of considerable hardship, the unwelcome Episcopalian clergy who had been forced upon them. This was called 'the rabbling of the curates.'

The cause for which the Covenanters had struggled was that of spiritual freedom. They wished religion to be independent of State control, and individuals to be free to obey their conscience. A favourite text was: "We ought to obey God rather than men" (Acts v. 29).

One of the dangers that beset the character of the later Covenanters was that of a bad sense of proportion. They were apt to be narrow-minded and bigoted and to let their feelings carry them away. On the other hand, they had convictions, and courage to uphold these, and zeal to maintain their cause. They had a simple faith based upon their reading of the Bible, and they lived an upright, disciplined life. Amongst those who disliked them may have been much of the culture of the time, a broader outlook and more self-restraint. But amongst their opponents were also the careless and licentious and irreligious, and all who detested such as set a high standard.

Scottish religion owes much to the freedom-loving spirit of the Covenanters. The position is well summed up by Thomas Carlyle in this exclamation: "How many earnest, rugged Cromwells, Knoxes, poor peasant Covenanters, wrestling, battling for very life, in rough, miry places, have to struggle and suffer and fall, greatly censured, bemired, before a beautiful Revolution of Eighty-eight can step over them in official pumps and silk-stockings, with universal three-times-three!"

Books to read:—

W. K. Hewison, 'The Covenanters.' (1913 edition.)
Wodrow, 'History of the Sufferings of the Church of Scotland.' (1835 edition.)
J. C. Johnston, 'Treasury of the Scottish Covenant.' (1887.)
H. Macpherson, 'The Covenanters under Persecution.' (1923.)

CHAPTER XII.

CHURCH LIFE IN THE SEVENTEENTH CENTURY.

WE have been dealing with major events in the history of Church and nation within Reformed Scotland, discussing the contribution of distinguished leaders and examining formative movements. It is, however, to be remembered that all the while the routine of religious life persisted. The thought and activities of the ordinary citizen often appear to be remarkably little affected by what seem to be epoch-making changes. Thus it is possible to give an account of the people's religion that will be generally true for practically the whole of the seventeenth century and the earlier part of the eighteenth. A development in the direction of Puritanism is certainly noticeable if one views this period as a whole, and one knows that in the history of a race no earnest thought, no suffering for conscience' sake, no devoted labour, can be in vain. Nevertheless, the alternating victory of Presbyterianism and Episcopacy within that time caused astonishingly small outward disturbance in most parishes. Let us interrupt our narrative, then, to inquire what religious practice was like in those days.

In Church.—The general principle behind church arrangements was that the laird or landowner in return for benefits received from the labour of the population was expected to provide them with houses, a mill, possibly a school, certainly a church and a minister with a stipend and manse. In the seventeenth century the people were still extremely poor and ignorant. The parish minister was, except during a short period, selected by the patron, and no other arrangement would have worked so satisfactorily. The minister was the people's adviser in spiritual matters and in much else. He would be the best educated man in the parish, occupied a good social position, and was expected to show an example to the people in Christian living. A pious, sensible, kindly minister would exercise a tremendous influence for good.

The minister had the advice of the elders. These were selected from different quarters of the parish as men thoroughly respected, who knew their Bibles, and who understood the people, and might be expected to watch over them both justly and mercifully.

The Kirk Session saw that the people came to church. A bell rang early on Sunday morning to get them out of bed, and soon to the clatter of the second bell they would be on their way to the early forenoon service. In certain periods the first part of the service was taken by the precentor, and at the third bell the minister entered in his dark gown and, mounting the pulpit, prayed and preached. The sermon was long, being timed by a half-hour glass in the pulpit. It was carefully prepared and delivered without paper, and required of the hearers some knowledge of the Bible and some taste for theology. Attacks on Rome and political questions of the moment were familiar subjects. The text of the sermon, except on special occasions, was a part of a Scripture passage which was called the 'ordinary,' and from this the minister preached Sunday after Sunday perhaps for months. The text was noted in the Session Minutes.

The churches could seldom be called handsome buildings, and the service was as bare and simple as the church. The psalms were sung by the sitting congregation without the aid of instrument or choir, the schoolmaster generally leading the praise from his precentor's desk below the pulpit, and having less than a dozen tunes at his command. The congregation stood during the prayers, which were long and biblical and extemporaneous. At the afternoon service the children might be catechised. For a long time in Scotland it was the custom for the minister in addition to the sermon to give a 'lecture,' this being an explanation of some chapter of the Bible instead of the mere reading of it. The regular collection was for the local poor, but sometimes there were special collections for the repair of harbours or bridges or the ransom of slaves.

The Sunday was very strictly observed both in Presbyterian

and in Episcopalian times. The Directory for the Public Worship of God says: "The whole day is to be celebrated as holy to the Lord, both in public and private, as being the Christian Sabbath. To which end, it is requisite that there be a holy cessation or resting all that day from all unnecessary labours, and an abstaining not only from all sports and pastimes, but also from all worldly words and thoughts." The Session supervised the doings of everyone, and individuals were frequently in trouble for working or trading or playing or travelling or fishing or drinking on the Lord's Day.

Baptism took place in church, a bowl of water being set in a ring attached to the pulpit. Marriages were also solemnised in church. In the case of burials there was no religious service at the grave. The Session provided a 'mortcloth' to cover the coffin, and sometimes a hand-bell to be rung as the funeral procession went along.

Communion was a very special occasion. The ordinance was generally observed only once a year. As the time approached, the minister went to every quarter of the parish and tested people's knowledge. Everyone had at least to know the Apostles' Creed, the Lord's Prayer, and the Ten Commandments. Everyone's behaviour was also reviewed. In one parish we read how "the minister intreats because the giving of Communion approacheth, that the elders be careful in their several quarters to search who are at variance and discord with their neighbours, and either reconcile them or else delate them to the Session, to the end those who are contumacious and will not be reconciled may be debarred from coming to the Table of the Lord."

Small 'tokens,' usually of lead, were given by the elders to all who proved satisfactory in conduct and knowledge, and on the appointed Sunday these were permitted in groups to take their turn at the long tables which were erected in the middle of the church, where they received the bread and the wine, distributed by the minister through the elders. Often Communion services were held on two consecutive Sundays, so that as many as possible might have a chance of being present. Members who removed from one parish to another were required to take testimonials with them from the Session.

In the eighteenth century Communion occasions brought people in large numbers from neighbouring parishes. We hear of hundreds bringing certificates of membership and being given 'tokens,' and having to be fed and housed for days. At such times the congregation gathered out of doors, the churches being much too small for the crowd. There was preaching from the 'tent,' and table after table was served, practically the whole day being occupied with preaching and the celebration of the Sacrament, and a number of ministers being present to share the burden of the services. In the seventeenth century the Sunday previous to Communion was usually a Fast Day or day of solemn preparation. Later, the Thursday before Communion was often so observed, and the Monday after Communion was a special day of Thanksgiving.

Among the People.—There were no Sunday Schools in those days. The children, however, were taught at school to sing the psalms, and they attended church with their parents, and could greatly help the praise. They were taught to read the Bible, this being one of the chief school books. After the Reformation the Geneva Bible was the translation used. Later, the Authorised Version of 1611 took its place. The children also learned Calvin's Catechism, or later the Shorter Catechism, and in this they might be examined at church. We hear how sometimes between the services one boy was put up to ask the Catechism questions and another to answer while the people listened. Children were questioned at home and at school on the subject of the sermon. Both they and older people often took an ink-horn and an exercise book to church and made notes of the sermon, and these notes were gone over round the fireside on Sunday evening.

At the close of the service in church the minister often gave a public rebuke to people who had been brought before the Session for wrong-doing. During the service these persons sat on what was called the 'stool of repentance.' If they were guilty of serious sin they would have to appear in public on several occasions before they were absolved and assured of God's forgiveness. In certain cases they would have to wear a sheet of sackcloth round them to prove their sorrow for what they had done.

The Kirk Session was not only concerned with the morals

of the parishioners, but had to try to put down superstition, such as making pilgrimages to supposed holy wells, or leaving a small corner of one's farm uncultivated as a bribe to the devil, or trying to work charms with a sieve and shears or with a key and a Bible. Everyone believed in witches, and the Session would sometimes have to examine a poor old woman whom the neighbours suspected of bewitching their cows or causing illness in the district. Quite a number were burnt to death as a result of such charges. The last case in Scotland was in 1727.

The Session also looked after the poor. The church collections were usually very small, for there was not much money in the country. Bad coins were also common, and often found their way to the church plate. But there was generally enough to provide for the deserving. People used to leave money to Sessions for the poor, and some parishes had considerable endowments of this sort. The blind, the maimed, the orphans and the widows, the mentally deficient, had to be supported by the Sessions. There was often trouble with able-bodied unemployed beggars, who terrorised the folks in lonely cottages, and Sessions might engage a sturdy man to keep such nuisances out of the parish. They might give badges to people as a licence to beg. Sir Walter Scott's Edie Ochiltree is drawn from such a case.

Family worship was encouraged by the Church, and was widely observed. A psalm was sung, Scripture read, and prayer offered. The General Assembly published in 1647 directions for worship in the home, and copies were distributed in the parishes by the elders. The best-known description of Scottish family worship is in Robert Burns's 'Cottar's Saturday Night,' and refers to the later eighteenth century.

The state of religion in the parish was watched by the Presbytery, which made regular visitations. On such occasions the minister was questioned regarding the elders, the schoolmaster, the beadle. The elders were asked about the minister, his character, preaching, visiting. Inquiries were made as to the condition of the church building, the provision made for the poor and for education, the services held, church attendance, the Communion vessels, the observance of Sacraments, and so on.

The Minister.—Preaching was thought to be very important. The true preaching of the Word of God, John Knox believed to be the chief evidence of a true Church. Knox himself was a stirring preacher. After him Master Robert Bruce (1554-1631) was the outstanding preacher in Edinburgh, and "shined as a great light through the whole land, the power and efficacy of the Spirit most sensibly accompanying the Word that he preached."

Seventeenth century ministers had a long college course, the lectures and exercises being in Latin and the studies dealing largely with Church controversies. This affected the sermons, which tended to be fully developed arguments with a multitude of heads. We are told that Scottish preachers "went all in one track of raising observations on points of 'doctrine' out of the text, and proving these by 'reasons,' and then of applying those, showing the 'use' that was to be made of such a point of doctrine, both for instruction and terror, for exhortation and comfort, for trial of themselves upon it, and for furnishing them with proper directions and helps, and this was so methodical that the people grew to follow a sermon quite through every branch of it." Not that nobody ever grew weary; we hear occasionally of the pole with which the beadle used to waken sleepers. There would be dull and ineffective preachers, as in all ages. 'Presbyterian Eloquence Displayed' (1692) is a sarcastic attack upon the sermons of the period. But the century had its share of outstanding men in its pulpits. It was a great preaching age both in England and in France, but Scotland also may be proud of its seventeenth century preachers.

To take only representative examples: David Dickson (died 1663) was a very rousing preacher, deeply emotional and intensely earnest. John Livingstone (died 1672), James Guthrie (executed 1661), and Samuel Rutherfurd (died 1661) were among the ardent upholders of the Covenants. William Guthrie (died 1665) was rather of the mystical type, a persuasive pleader for the Gospel. Andrew Gray (died 1656) was a preacher who crowded the Inner High Church of Glasgow. James Durham (died 1658) of the Outer High had not the same popularity, but there was more in his sermons. One of the greatest of all was Hew Binning (died 1653), who was quite a young man when he died, but has left us proof in his writings of intellect and originality and personal spiritual experience. Amongst Episcopalian preachers we may mention William Cowper, Bishop of Galloway (died 1619), James Sibbald, one of the Aberdeen Doctors (died in Ireland, 1647), and, of course, Robert Leighton (died 1684), and his friends James Nairn (died 1678) and Laurence Charteris (died 1700). Nor must we forget the field preachers of the later Covenanting times.

There were others whose writings were a strength and a credit to the Church of Scotland. George Hutcheson (died 1674) of Edinburgh, James Fergusson of Kilwinning (died 1667) were, along with David Dickson and James Durham, very capable expositors of Scripture. Theologians of massive learning included Robert Boyd (died 1627) and John Forbes of Corse (died 1648). The controversial writers were numerous and extremely erudite. George Gillespie of Wemyss (died 1648) and his brother Patrick (died 1675), who was Principal of Glasgow University, may be taken as representative. Historical works by David Calderwood (died 1650) the Presbyterian, and John Spottiswoode (died 1639) the Episcopalian, and others, remain of value. A book such as 'Naphtali' (1667) or 'A Hind Let Loose' (1687) admits us to the innermost heart of the persecuted Covenanters. Of an entirely different type is that truly devotional little book 'The Life of God in the Soul of Man,' by Henry Scougall, the youthful professor at Aberdeen (died 1678). The century also saw the publication of an extraordinary number of pamphlets by ministers of the Church of Scotland. Sermons, too, were published in large numbers. There can be no doubt that the ministers in this period had something to say, and had the power to express themselves. Taken as a whole, the literature we have indicated is not of extremely high literary quality, and most of it has ceased to interest any but scholars. At the same time it was evidence of keen interest and wonderful diligence and strong conviction.

Contacts with the Continent.—It is to be noted that the Church of Scotland in this century did not struggle away in isolation. It was in close touch with Protestant churches elsewhere, and was influenced for good by these contacts. Many Scots studied in France in the early part of the century, and Dutch thought was extremely familiar later, while English Puritanism made a deep and permanent impression upon Scottish religion. There was a unity amongst Protestants in those days due in part to their common interest in the Bible, to their common use of the Latin language, and to the universities which supplied their common thought. Nor must we overlook their common dread of Rome. The Scots were in direct contact with the Reformed Churches of Switzerland, France, Holland, Hungary, and other lands. This was important and healthy for all, and it was most unfortunate that in later times the contacts diminished so seriously. At no period can Scottish history be properly understood unless it is carefully studied as a part of European history, and this is quite markedly true of the seventeenth century.

Books to read :—

G. D. Henderson, 'Religious Life in Seventeenth Century Scotland.' (1937.)

G. D. Henderson, 'The Scottish Ruling Elder.' (1935.)

CHAPTER XIII.

THE REVOLUTION SETTLEMENT.

Presbyterianism Restored.—The Revolution Settlement of 1690 restored Presbyterianism in Scotland. A strong reaction against the determined absolutism and aggressive Romanism of James II. brought William and Mary to the throne. It was natural that they should wish to continue the arrangement that had now existed for a generation under which Episcopacy was the one recognised form of Christianity throughout the whole kingdom. Uniformity had much to commend it. On the other hand, William had been brought up in Holland in a Church that was very similar to that of Scotland under Presbyterianism. Further, his chief adviser on Scottish religious affairs was William Carstares (1649-1715), a whole-hearted Presbyterian.

Carstares, son of a minister who suffered persecution at the hands of the Episcopalians, studied at Edinburgh and then at Utrecht in Holland, where, like many others, he found the safety which Scotland could no longer offer him. He became a favourite with William of Orange, and remained in his confidence for over thirty years. More than once he suffered imprisonment in Britain as a result of government suspicions, being subjected on one occasion to torture by 'thumbkins.' Crossing with William's expedition in 1688, he continued his sagacious counsel and intimate friendship till the monarch's death. His influence was so powerful that he was nicknamed 'Cardinal' Carstares. Becoming Principal of Edinburgh University, he took an important share in the negotiations for the Union of Parliaments of 1707, and was four times Moderator of the General Assembly. Not only was he wise and statesmanlike, but he possessed a sound character, a devout nature, and a kind heart.

The prospects in Scotland at the Revolution were also affected by the fact that the Scottish Episcopalians, with their belief in the Divine Right of Kings, mostly remained faithful to the Stuarts. Only a few days before William landed in England, the Scottish bishops wrote to James II. declaring their "firm and unshaken loyalty"; and when in an interview the new monarch asked for an assurance of the allegiance of the Scottish Episcopalians he received a very non-committal answer; they would, it was said, support him "so far as law, reason, or conscience would allow."

Such was the general feeling in Scotland itself that the Convention of Estates, consisting of nobles, gentry, burgesses, and higher clergy, when it met in April 1689, in the Claim of Right by which it offered the throne of Scotland to William and Mary, stipulated that Episcopacy should be abolished as "a great and insupportable grievance and trouble to this nation, and contrary to the inclinations of the generality of the people, ever since the Reformation (they having reformed from Popery by Presbyters)."

The new sovereign agreed to "settle by law that Church government in this kingdom which is most agreeable to the inclinations of the people," and accordingly Episcopacy was set aside, and the Presbyterian system of 1592 was revived. 'Outed' ministers were restored, the Westminster Confession was confirmed, and the first meeting of General Assembly since 1653 was summoned for 3rd October 1690. The Stuart theory that the king was "supreme over all persons and in all causes, civil and ecclesiastical," was explicitly repudiated.

Presbyterianism was not officially declared to be the one divinely instituted form of Church government. There was no suggestion of the Divine Right of Presbytery. It was only said that most of the people wanted it. Further, there was no mention whatever of the Covenants. The Cameronians were, of course, sorely disappointed with this attitude, and some of their descendants in consequence still hold aloof from the Church of Scotland.

James II. had now been dethroned for the very reasons which the Cameronians had stated against his accession and for maintaining which they had suffered. Although they did not obtain all that their extreme leaders would have liked, it is very plain that but for their sheer obstinacy in maintaining at all costs under the most testing conditions the cause of Presbyterianism, there would have been no Revolution Settlement.

Religious Toleration.—King William insisted upon toleration. "I will not," he said, "lay myself under any obligation to be a persecutor." In his letter to the General Assembly of 1690 he said: "We could never be of the mind that violence was suited to the advancing of true religion. . . . Moderation is what religion enjoins, neighbouring churches expect from you, and we recommend to you."

Toleration had not hitherto been an outstanding virtue of either Presbyterians or Episcopalians. They thought a belief must be either 'right' or 'wrong,' and failed to recognise that it might be merely 'better' or 'worse.' They would have agreed that there should be "unity in things necessary, liberty in things indifferent," and possibly they might have added "and in all things charity"; but they could never agree as to what things were really 'necessary,' and they generally acted as if no points could be more essential than those upon which they differed from their neighbours. A more enlightened view was beginning to be expressed. John Locke, the English philosopher, wrote in 1689: "Absolute liberty, just and true liberty, is the thing that we stand in need of." He even ventured to declare: "No man is hurt because his neighbour is of a different religion from his own, and no civil society is hurt because its members are of different religions from one another." The Revolution Settlement could not therefore take the attitude adopted at the Reformation Settlement of 1567, when Parliament asserted that "there is no other face of kirk nor other face of religion than is presently by the favour of God established within this realm."

At first there was some vindictiveness, not perhaps unnatural, on the part of men who had suffered from persecution and exile; but presently a calmer attitude prevailed, and patient treatment of the humiliated Episcopalians became the rule. The parishes, indeed, of about two hundred of the unpopular 'curates' in the South-West of Scotland who had been rabbled were declared vacant, while any minister who had been 'outed' by the Episcopalians was restored, the Episcopalian occupant of the charge being ejected. But such as were willing to declare their allegiance to William and Mary were allowed to remain where they were, and many did so. In a considerable number of parishes the Episcopalian minister continued his old form of service (which indeed differed little from that of his Presbyterian neighbour) till his death perhaps a quarter of a century later. In the North-East of Scotland the great mass of the ministers were Episcopalian, and the people were generally content to have it so, with the result that even those who were hostile to King William continued in office by popular consent, in spite of Parliament and General Assembly. Some actually prayed regularly for James as king; and any attempt to put a Presbyterian in their place was met by a mob armed with stones and divots. Some who were ejected from parishes held services in meeting-houses. Presbyterianism was just as unpopular in this part of the country as Episcopacy was in the South-West or in Fife, and it was many years before it was well organised. No Presbyterian Communion service could be held in the town of Aberdeen till 1704. In Moray and Ross the conditions were somewhat similar.

In some other places, such as Edinburgh, small Episcopalian meeting-houses were erected, and so long as the clergy did not attempt to exercise the rights of a parish minister they were generally unmolested. The number of professing Episcopalians, except in special districts, was not large.

Queen Anne, who came to the throne in 1702, was well disposed to the Episcopalians, and they were able to obtain from the British Parliament in 1712 an Act of Toleration to prevent such misunderstandings and unpleasant incidents as had occasionally occurred, and to make their position clear and secure. Their use of the Anglican Book of Common Prayer was legalised. They were now a recognised separate sect alongside the Church of Scotland. This small Scottish Episcopal Church was unfortunately soon much affected by internal disputes, and it was even more shaken as a result of the active part taken by its clergy and members in the Jacobite Rebellions of 1715 and 1745 and the consequent political restrictions laid upon them.

William and Mary did not win the support of all Scotland. Romanists and Episcopalians were against them, and this opposition flared up in the short rebellion headed by Graham of Claverhouse, "Bonnie Dundee," one of those figures in Scottish history so much over-praised by friends and over-blamed by enemies.

"To the Lords of Convention, 'twas Claverhouse spoke,
'Ere the King's crown go down, there are crowns to be broke.'"

This leader was victorious at Killiecrankie (1689), but was killed in the battle, and his Highland supporters were soon afterwards defeated at Dunkeld by the regiment which had been formed from among the Cameronians. These Cameronians had a Bible as a regulation part of their kit. The regiment has continued to hold an honoured place in the British Army.

Church Worship and Government in the New Order.—The Presbyterians of the early eighteenth century were more puritan than those of the late sixteenth. They very naturally wished to distinguish themselves sharply from the Episcopalians in their worship. Hence the pronounced dislike for anything of forms and ceremonies. They were further than ever from the use of a printed liturgy, even such as that of Knox, and less ritualistic than their Calvinistic brethren in other lands. In the baptismal service there was a reference to the Westminster Confession instead of that repetition of the Apostles' Creed which was a reminder that by baptism one becomes a member not of a particular sect, but of the Christian Church. There was even an increased antipathy to the Lord's Prayer in public worship, though Calvin and Knox regularly employed it and the Directory of 1645 recommended it. The 'lecture' in place of simple reading of Scripture had come in from English practice. So had the 'reading of the line' in the metrical psalms, which one still hears in certain Gaelic-speaking districts, but which had been allowed by the Directory of 1645 only "for the present, where many of the congregation cannot read."

The government of the Church was, of course, by General Assembly, Synods, Presbyteries, and Kirk Sessions in accordance with the provisions of 1592. The first Assembly consisted simply of the sixty survivors of those ministers who had been 'outed' in 1662, with ministers who had accepted the Indulgences, and a body of elders including noblemen, lairds, and magistrates.

Some useful work was done by General Assemblies during this period. The famous Barrier Act, which is still part of the law of the Church, was passed in 1697. It ensures that a serious alteration in Church matters cannot simply be carried and made law at the Assembly at which it is first brought up. The proposal must be sent down to Presbyteries for their consideration and report. The Church has a year to think over the matter thoroughly, and then the next General Assembly in the light of the discussion that has taken place decides whether or not to pass the measure and bring the change into force. The Act provides a useful check against hasty action.

The first Assembly after the Revolution had taken up the needs of Gaelic-speaking districts, and the Assembly by 1694 was in a position to order the use of a Gaelic version of the metrical psalms and of the Shorter Catechism. The Assembly of 1704 gave its blessing to the scheme for the Society for the Propagation of Christian Knowledge, which was established a few years later and began a most beneficent work in the Highlands and Islands of Scotland, providing schools and missionaries in large scattered parishes.

The National Church.—The Assembly in the last years of the century showed concern with regard to the exceedingly bad condition of trade and the increase of poverty throughout the country. The Darien Scheme for a Scottish trade colony in America was meant to be the beginning of a more prosperous time, and the Assembly asked for the people's prayers for its success. The undertaking, however, was hopelessly mismanaged, and failed completely, so that things were worse than ever. It became clear that better times could only come through closer union with England. Union was felt to be essential to Scotland for commercial reasons and to England for political reasons. There was increasing bitterness of ill-feeling between Scotland and England, and the only remedy was either complete union or complete separation, and of these possibilities the former was plainly the more hopeful.

As an act of necessity the Union received the reluctant support of the Church, led by the discerning and far-sighted Carstares. But had the Church not first been assured that there would be no interference with the religious liberties secured by the Revolution Settlement, there would have been no Union. The Act of Security incorporated in the Act of Union made this a condition of entering into negotiations with England. By the Act of Union in 1707 the continuance of the Westminster doctrine and Presbyterian Church government of the National Church was thus guaranteed, and it was stipulated that each new sovereign immediately upon accession shall promise to 'maintain and preserve' the Church of Scotland, its government, worship, discipline, right, and privileges.

When the Union was at last accomplished, the Scottish Chancellor is reported to have remarked, "There is an end of an old song." It certainly was the end of some features of Scottish independence and the beginning of greatly increased English influence; but we must remember—though it is often overlooked by outsiders—that Scotland retained, and retains, its religious independence and its National Presbyterian Church.

The ministers of this period, like those of others, varied in type and quality. A good example may be found in Thomas Boston of Ettrick (1676-1732), whose 'Memoirs' show him busy with his few commentaries and his Hebrew Old Testament, making notes in his Commonplace Book, studying his lectures and sermons to be delivered without paper, preaching the Gospel with strong emotion and utter conviction insisting on men's need of Christ, holding little prayer meetings, or leading family worship, or engaged in the most earnest private prayer, or writing out for himself a private covenant with God, deeply impressed by the evidences of God's presence with him, and also by the deceits and activities of Satan, visiting his parishioners in sickness or trouble or to instruct them by catechising, discussing the problems of the day with his brethren of the Presbytery, observing congregational fast-days, or celebrating Communion with eager crowds of his own parishioners and others. Boston's writings became extremely popular, being widely read, not only in Scotland but in Holland, for a century and a half after his death. The best known is his 'Fourfold State' (1720), with its plain doctrinal statement and homely religious appeal.

Most of the other writers of this period dealt rather with the question of Church government, which was still so much in the public mind. There was a flood of pamphlets ; and the books of Gilbert Rule, Thomas Forrester, William Jameson, John Anderson, and others appeared in defence of Presbyterianism, while such authors as George Garden and Thomas Rhind upheld the Episcopalian standpoint.

Books to read :—

R. H. Story, 'William Carstares.' (1874.)
'Memoirs of Thomas Boston.' (Morrison's edition.)

CHAPTER XIV.

THE FIRST SECESSION.

THE Church of Scotland in the early eighteenth century included all sections of the people except, on the one extreme, the relatively small group of Romanists and Episcopalians and, on the other, the Cameronians. But within this national unity all were not of one type. The difference of temperament and outlook which had formerly distinguished the Resolutioner from the Protester persisted, and it now produced the parties known as Moderates and Evangelicals.

The difference showed itself in connection with several matters. The chief of these were Theology, the relation of Church and State, the Patronage question, and the problem of authority and the individual conscience.

Theological Differences.—In Theology, 'the science of things divine,' the Moderates inclined to a formal adherence to the generally accepted system, or else to freer thinking amounting in some cases almost to Rationalism, that view of the world which leaves no room for the supernatural. They themselves would have said that they were broad-minded. Those on the other side regarded them as lax and careless in their beliefs, if not actually erroneous or heretical.

The Evangelical party included those who were strict, orthodox, traditional Calvinists, and those who laid a particular emphasis upon the free offer of the Gospel to all. Their opponents thought them obscurantist, narrow, and over-enthusiastic.

Trouble arose about the teaching of Professor John Simson of Glasgow University, who had the kind of mind that likes adventure in thinking, and was not content to expound the details of an already complete system. He had been impressed by the open-mindedness of the Arminians, followers of the Dutch teacher Arminius (died 1609), who were strong opponents of Calvinism. Later he became interested in English works connected with the new movement of thought that became so influential in the eighteenth century throughout Europe, and that goes by the name of the Enlightenment—a movement inspired by belief in the power of human reason, and therefore inclined to think of Jesus Christ rather as a great teacher than as the Saviour. Simson was first accused of Arminianism in 1714, and after some years of controversy the Assembly contented itself with advising him to be more careful about what he said. But suspicion remained, and the matter was reopened in 1726, when he was accused of Arian heresy (teaching scarcely consistent with the doctrine of the divinity of Christ), and, after a lengthy inquiry, suspended in 1729 from teaching. The 'Simson affair' is of importance as revealing, on the one hand, the beginnings of a desire to think out theological problems in a scientific way apart from tradition. This was strengthened by the teaching of Francis Hutcheson, the philosopher (died 1746), and became a feature of the century. It is also of importance as having brought out the Evangelical conviction that men of Simson's stamp are dangerous to the Church, and the party's perturbation when the Assembly did not deal more severely with the culprit.

Trouble further arose over the teaching of the Evangelical 'Marrow Men.' In 1645 there had appeared the first part of a book by an English Puritan, Edward Fisher, entitled 'The Marrow of Modern Divinity.' When Thomas Boston, somewhere about 1700, was visiting a parishioner he discovered in the house a copy of this book, and found its doctrine of Grace most satisfying. The General Assembly of 1717 was asked to judge of a complaint by William Craig to whom the Presbytery of Auchterarder had refused an extract of his licence as a preacher of the Gospel, because he hesitated to sign the statement "that it is not sound and orthodox to teach that we must forsake sin in order to our coming to Christ." The action of the Presbytery in requiring signature of this 'Auchterarder Creed' was condemned by the Assembly. The Presbytery wished to make sure that the young man held the true faith, and meant merely that we come to Christ just as we are, in order to be purified and forgiven; but their words might be held to imply that one could accept Christ and go on living in sin.

Thomas Boston and others agreed with the Auchterarder view, which was exactly that of the 'Marrow of Modern Divinity,' and in 1718 James Hog of Carnock published a new edition of that work. It was condemned by the Assembly in 1720, but in 1721 twelve ministers signed a 'representation' against this decision. These 'Marrow Men' included Boston and Hog and Ebenezer and Ralph Erskine. The Assembly of 1722 censured them, and they protested. This controversy is of importance as showing these Evangelicals stressing feeling and religion, while their opponents emphasised reason and conduct. The difference between the attitudes is marked.

Church and State.—Turning to the question of Church and State, we remember that at the Revolution Settlement Scotland had escaped from the doctrine of royal supremacy in Church matters. It had not, however, escaped from State interference with religion. There are different ways in which Church and State may be related, from the one extreme of Erastianism (from Thomas Erastus, a Swiss, died 1583) which puts religion entirely under State control, to the views of Anabaptists and Independents that a Church is simply a group of persons with whose religious meetings and opinions the State has no concern. We have noted the ideas of Calvin and Andrew Melville. Most of the troubles of the Church in Scotland in the seventeenth century were due to this problem of the connection between Church and State; and the demand for spiritual freedom lay behind the Secessions of 1733 and 1761 and the Disruption of 1843.

The Revolution Settlement itself rested upon the action of Parliament in declaring Presbyterianism re-established in Scotland. After the Union of 1707 Parliament interfered very definitely in two instances. The first was the Toleration Act of 1712, which directly affected certain rights and privileges of the Church. The second, which had more unpleasant results, was the Patronage Act of 1712. It was not wanted by the Church. It was known to be largely the work of Jacobite Episcopalians. It was likely to weaken especially the Evangelical party. It seemed to be a breach of the Treaty of Union. But the main point of note is that, in passing this Act, the State was forcing its will upon the Church.

Patronage.—The Patronage question itself became the immediate cause of the Secessions. It had from early times been the natural practice that landowners, who had the responsibility of building the churches and paying the clergy, should also select the men who were to do the work. The Church stipulated that the choice must be from amongst those whom it recognised as qualified. At the same time it was always admitted that the consent of the people directly or indirectly was an element in the election process. Democratic ideas with regard to the rights of individuals such as are commonplace with us were not thought of until comparatively modern times. Patronage had actually been abolished in 1649, restored in 1661, and again abolished in 1690; but politics had much to do with these changes, as also with the Act of 1712.

There were now, however, a good many persons in the Church who held as a matter of principle that "the Christian people or society of believers who join in full Communion together are the persons who, according to the New Testament, have a right to elect their minister." This assumed a view of the Church like that of the English Independents, but it also showed amongst Church people a deepened personal interest which deserved to be fostered and encouraged. That people should desire more responsibility is healthy.

In practice the new Patronage Act did not at first create much trouble. In burghs the Town Council was patron and might be said to represent the people. In about a third of the country parishes the Crown was patron, and made a habit of consulting local opinion. Many other patrons acted similarly. But from about 1725 there was an increase in the number of cases where ministers whom the people did not wish to have were thrust upon them. In 1729 a new scheme was adopted whereby, when the local Presbytery was unwilling to induct such a man on account of the popular feeling, the Assembly sent a 'riding committee' to over-ride the local court and carry through the necessary proceedings.

The Assembly in 1731 attempted to lessen the causes of complaint by the proposal that in cases where the patron had not exercised his right of appointment, the Protestant heritors and the elders "who represent the people" shall "elect and call one to be their minister whom they are to propose to the whole congregation to be either approven or disapproven by them." This overture was sent down to Presbyteries under the Barrier Act; but the answers received were open to different interpretations, and both those in favour of the proposal and its opponents claimed to have a majority of the Presbyteries on their side. After heated debate the Assembly of 1732 passed the Act. The opposition was upon the ground that the Act did not go far enough because it failed to give to congregations the right of electing their own ministers. The leader of the dissatisfied party was Ebenezer Erskine, who thus became the champion of the people's rights.

The Seceders.—Ebenezer Erskine (1680-1754), son of a persecuted Covenanter, became minister of Portmoak and later at Stirling. He was much influenced by the deeply religious nature of his wife. His preaching attracted crowds, especially at Communion seasons. The sermons were full of Bible references, and centred round the offer of free grace. He was of a dignified, cold type, intense and conscientious, righteous and devout, judging sternly, not broad-minded, but a man of strong convictions and a determined leader.

At a Synod at Perth in 1732 he preached from the text, "The stone which the builders refused is become the head-stone of the corner" (Psalm cviii. 22), and took the opportunity of attacking the Assembly for respect of persons, for denying the people their rights, and for endangering spiritual freedom. The Synod rebuked him for expressions likely to disturb the peace of the Church and for assailing its highest court. He appealed to the General Assembly in 1733, but that body agreed with the Synod. Erskine was supported by William Wilson of Perth (died 1741), Alexander Moncrieff of Abernethy (died 1761), and James Fisher of Kinclaven (died 1775), all earnest, saintly, and faithful ministers. The four handed in a protest whose wording caused further irritation, but which they refused to withdraw. The Commission of Assembly was instructed to deal severely with the four protesters if they continued stubborn; and they were accordingly suspended from performing their ministerial duties, and when they still remained obdurate they were declared to be no longer ministers of the Church of Scotland.

Undoubtedly they were treated with quite unnecessary harshness. The situation was mishandled. The Church had no Alexander Henderson or William Carstares to guide it. Strong representations in favour of Erskine and his friends were made by Evangelicals throughout the country, and the Assembly of 1734 annulled an Act of 1730 which refused the registering of reasons of dissent and which had been responsible for some of the trouble; the Act of 1732, which had been the chief matter of dispute; and the Act depriving the four protesters of their status. Erskine and the others were left in possession of their churches, manses, and stipends until 1740, when, it being obvious that they were not prepared to yield, they were at last deposed.

In November 1733 the four subscribed a protestation that they adhered to the principles of the true, Presbyterian, covenanted Church of Scotland, and were in communion particularly with all affected with the grievances of which they had complained, and stating that they found themselves obliged to make a Secession, but appealed to "the first free, faithful, and reforming General Assembly of the Church of Scotland." On 5th December 1733 they met at Gairney Bridge, near Kinross, and there the Associate Presbytery (later Associate Synod) was formed.

It may be wondered why the Seceders did not return to the Church of Scotland when it approached them in a repentant spirit in 1734 and later. But it has to be borne in mind that although certain actions rising from the Act of 1732 were the immediate cause of the Secession, they were not the ultimate cause. The Seceders represented a type that was particularly unhappy and impatient in the company of the Moderates. This is clear from the Judicial Testimony issued by the Associate Presbytery in 1736, where they declare their dissatisfaction with the spirit of toleration in the Church, and the want of severity in dealing with erroneous doctrine such as that of John Simson; with the abandonment of the Covenants which were the charter of spiritual freedom, and the acceptance of establishment by the State in 1690, and the State's Toleration Act of 1712; with the submission to Patronage; and with the tyranny of the Church over the freedom of conscience of such as desired to testify against the faults of the Church, as did Erskine in his Synod sermon.

Here then we have the causes of separation—the trend of theology, Church and State, Patronage, and, finally, the relation of the Church's authority to the individual conscience, a matter to which further attention must be called in connection with the Second Secession.

In 1737 the Associate Presbytery was strengthened by the addition of two new Seceders, Thomas Mair of Orwell and Ralph Erskine of Dunfermline. The latter (died 1752) was a younger brother of Ebenezer, equally devout and earnest, but of a more genial nature and with more versatile powers, an interesting writer and preacher, highly emotional, fond of his violin, and with a certain poetic gift. His 'Gospel Sonnets' were popular. One poem was entitled 'Smoking Spiritualised.' A verse of it runs:—

> "Was this small plant for thee cut down ?
> So was the Plant of great renown,
> Which mercy sends
> For nobler ends :
> Thus think, and smoke tobacco."

Separatist Zeal.—The Associate Presbytery found that in many districts throughout Scotland there were groups discontented with the spiritual food that was being provided for them by the parish minister. They undertook to supply the needs of these groups as far as possible. Students were trained for the ministry, and settled where there was a demand. Some of the new churches had to serve a large area, and people walked long distances to the services. In some places Praying Societies had to be left to carry on as best they could for a time. Lay elders found an opportunity of giving special service, and in the new church acquired a position of larger influence than had been assigned them by the practice of the Church of Scotland. Congregations which wished to have an ordained minister had to make suitable provision for his maintenance. In Glasgow and some other places the increase of population, the failure of the Church of Scotland to erect new churches to meet the needs of the times, and the development of democratic ideas created a field of opportunity for the Associate Presbytery. In some places a local quarrel or misunderstanding could now be rendered less hurtful by the formation of a new congregation. The Associate leaders made no attempt, as did the Free Church later, to have a church in every parish.

Thomas Carlyle praises the Seceders. "Very venerable are these old seceding clergy to me when I look back on them." "A man who awoke to the belief that he actually had a soul to be saved or lost was apt to be found among the dissenting people."

Unfortunately their very earnestness and zeal led them to unhappy disputes and to an exaggerated idea of the importance of small differences. Amidst much bitterness the Synod in 1747 split into Burghers and Anti-Burghers, the latter being the stricter sect, disapproving the terms of an oath in which the burgesses of certain towns declared their adherence to "the true religion presently professed within this realm." Ebenezer Erskine was excommunicated by the Anti-Burghers. Their leader was Adam Gib (died 1788), a fierce controversialist, deeply versed in seventeenth century theology, an enthusiast who signed a covenant with God in his own blood.

The Burghers further divided into Old Lights and New Lights in 1799, and a similar split took place amongst the Anti-Burghers in 1806. Ultimately these several sundered parts came together again almost completely to form the United Secession Church of 1820, which in 1847 became part of the United Presbyterian Church.

Books to read :—

A. R. MacEwen, 'The Erskines.' (Famous Scots Series.)
J. M'Kerrow, 'History of the Secession Church.' (1839.)
H. Grey Graham, 'Social Life of Scotland in the Eighteenth Century.'

CHAPTER XV.

THE SECOND SECESSION AND THE MODERATES.

The Spread of Discontent.—The Second Secession dates from 1761. Its general causes were similar to those which produced the First Secession. Patrons had for some time been more insistent upon their rights to present ministers to vacant charges. To the many parishes in the gift of the Crown, the government, under the advice of Argyll (died 1761), was appointing Moderates. Other patrons were convinced that by exercising their rights they obtained a more cultured and gentlemanly type of minister than when they left the election to local parties. Patrons had also been stiffened in defence of their rights by the attempt of the Church in 1750 to secure a general increase of stipends in view of the great and permanent change that had taken place in the cost of living. The heritors through their influence with Parliament managed to defeat this effort; but it could scarcely be expected that they would relish the double demand, that they should pay more towards stipend, and that at the same time they should give up the privilege of selecting the man whom they were to pay.

Feeling in favour of popular election had been strengthened by a number of appointments which had given peculiar offence to parishioners. Mob riots, bitter legal disputes, difference of opinion in Presbyteries did anything but spread the Christian spirit through the land. The 'riding committees' satisfied the law, but gave no other satisfaction.

There had been a long and disturbed vacancy at Torphichen, but at last the Assembly decided that a certain minister had been duly elected, and instructed the Presbytery of Linlithgow to induct him. The Presbytery refused on grounds of conscience. At the Assembly of 1751 John Home moved and William Robertson seconded that the members of the Presbytery be suspended; but this was defeated by a very large majority, and a 'riding committee' was appointed as formerly. By next Assembly the position was changed. The Torphichen 'riding committee' was the last.

A vacancy had occurred at Inverkeithing, and a minister was duly presented; but there was so much popular opposition that the Presbytery of Dunfermline would not induct him. At the Assembly of 1752 William Robertson moved, not that the issue be avoided by a 'riding committee' taking over the responsibility of the Presbytery, but that the Presbytery itself be ordered to admit the presentee on a certain date and to report on the following day to the Assembly, which would still be in session. Opinion had altered definitely since last Assembly, and Robertson easily carried his motion. The usual quorum of a Presbytery was three, but it was known that three of the Dunfermline Presbytery were willing to act, and therefore the number was on this occasion specially raised to five, so that it might be a test case, and some who were unwilling would be forced to choose whether they would obey the Assembly or obey what they believed to be their conscience. Robertson's point was that if the decisions of a Higher Court may be disobeyed by Presbyteries or ministers, that is the end of Presbyterianism. General Assemblies may as well cease to meet. Discipline no longer exists, and discipline is the essence of the Presbyterian system. The constitution of the Church is ruined by abuse of liberty. Those on the other side stood out for the rights of the individual conscience against the authority even of the Assembly, and held that this was of the essence of Reformation teaching. It was a question of law or freedom, both vital to a healthy society.

When the appointed day arrived there were only three members of the Presbytery in attendance at Inverkeithing. Six were absent; and the General Assembly, by way of making an example and to assert its authority, decided to depose one of these. Thomas Gillespie of Carnock (1708-1774) was by a very large majority selected to suffer this punishment. He was accordingly deposed from the ministry of the Church of Scotland and his charge declared vacant. When he heard the sentence, he said that he received it "with real concern and awful impressions of the divine conduct in it," but that he rejoiced that to him it was "given on behalf of Christ, not only to believe on Him but also to suffer for His sake."

The Relief Church.—Gillespie had received part of his education at Edinburgh University with a view to the ministry of the Church of Scotland. Before his course was finished, however, he went to study under William Wilson of Perth, who was preparing students for the Associate Presbytery; but he was dissatisfied with his experience and left after ten days. He eventually completed his training under Dr Doddridge, an English Independent, at Northampton, and was ordained by a group of ministers there. When he returned to Scotland his ordination was not called in question, and he became minister of Carnock in 1741. He was clearly a man with a mind of his own, not deeply concerned about the law and tradition of the Church of Scotland, but anxious for an effective Gospel ministry. Without being in any way brilliant, Gillespie was a very faithful and respected minister and a good man.

When he returned home after his deposition he told his wife: "I am no longer minister of Carnock"; and her worthy reply was: "Well, if we must beg, I will carry the meal-poke." For a time he preached in the open air, but presently a church was built for him in Dunfermline, where his ministry attracted much attention as that of one who had suffered for refusing to do what he believed to be wrong. At last in 1761 he and two other ministers of congregations which had broken with the Church of Scotland because of election disputes formed themselves into the Presbytery of Relief. Other congregations grew up. Students for the ministry were at first trained in the Divinity Halls of the Universities along with the Church of Scotland students. By 1847, when the Relief Church became part of the United Presbyterian Church, it had 136 congregations.

The Relief Church claimed to exist for the "relief of Christians oppressed in their Christian privileges." It was strongly Evangelical, but was opposed to the fondness of the Associate Synod for the Covenants; held, like the English Independents, that the civil magistrate had no concern with religion; and showed unusual liberality for that period in being ready to admit to Communion members of any denomination.

Although numbers of Evangelical ministers and people were thus slipping away from the Church of Scotland, there still remained an influential Evangelical party within that Church. George Whitefield, a Church of England Calvinistic evangelist, fellow-labourer with the Wesleys, came to Scotland in 1741 intending to co-operate with the Associate Presbytery, but soon found that impossible, and proceeded to work under the auspices of Church of Scotland Evangelical ministers. The revival which began at Cambuslang in 1742 and spread to many parts of the country was supported by ministers and members of the Church of Scotland. John Wesley paid repeated visits to Scotland and preached in many Scottish pulpits, though the fact that he was not a Calvinist interfered greatly with his success. The Church of Scotland could boast such an enthusiastic Evangelical as John Willison of Dundee (died 1750), whose writings long remained popular.

In the succeeding period the most interesting figure in the party was probably John Erskine of Greyfriars Church, Edinburgh (1721-1803), who has been described by Scott in 'Guy Mannering.' Lord Cockburn in his 'Memorials' says: "Dr John Erskine! How everybody reverenced him! Though able and well-read, his reputation rested on the better basis of a fine spirit, operating in all the walks in which liberal religion and active benevolence can be engaged." He spoke "good, honest, natural Scotch."

The Moderates.—But with the victory of William Robertson at the Assembly of 1752 began the period of Moderate domination within the Church. Scotland was prosperous in the second half of the eighteenth century, and the level of culture rose distinctly. Voltaire could write that "at the present time it is from Scotland we receive rules of taste in all the arts from the Epic poem to gardening." Smollett, the Scottish novelist (1721-1771), could speak of Edinburgh in his later life as a "hot-bed of genius." It was the period in which flourished David Hume (1711-1776), one of the world's great philosophers; Adam Smith (1723-1790), amongst the foremost figures in the history of Economics; Henry Raeburn, the painter (1756-1823); Robert Burns (1759-1796),

Scotland's favourite poet. Moderates who were ministers of the Church of Scotland added greatly to their country's reputation.

William Robertson (1721-1793) was from 1762 Principal of Edinburgh University, and for many years the leader of his party and the controlling influence in the Church. A good student, a hard-working parish minister, an outstanding member of Edinburgh society at its most celebrated period, a man of character, principle, and personality, he became famous as a historian. His 'History of Scotland,' his 'Charles V.,' and other works had a flattering reception even in England and on the Continent. King George III., Horace Walpole, Edward Gibbon, and everyone else read and praised them. Cockburn describes Robertson as he had seen him: "A pleasant looking old man, with an eye of great vivacity and intelligence, a large projecting chin, a small hearing trumpet . . . and a rather large wig, powdered and curled." Like everyone else at the time, Robertson had a broad Scots accent. His Evangelical colleague, John Erskine, praises his sagacity, independence of judgment, exemplary character, skilful leadership of men, and persuasive eloquence in debate.

Thomas Reid (1710-1796), the outstanding member of the Scottish School of Philosophy, taught at Aberdeen and Glasgow Universities. His acute intellect did much to stem the tide of the scepticism for which Hume was responsible.

Hugh Blair (1718-1800), Professor of Rhetoric at Edinburgh, was the best-known preacher of his day. His published sermons were read to the king. Samuel Johnson, who did not like things Scottish, admitted that he had gone through them "with more than approbation," and they were fashionable everywhere. To us they seem to be rather tasteful, stylish, Christian moral discourses than sermons. They treated of such subjects as Envy, Patience, Duties belonging to middle age, Idleness, Extremes in religion and morality. They were typical of the refinement of the time.

William Wilkie of Ratho (1721-1772) may be mentioned as the author of a long epic poem on a classical subject which brought him the title of 'the Scottish Homer,' and for very enterprising agricultural work which more suitably earned for him the name of 'Potato Wilkie.' Thomas Blacklock (1721-1791), a probationer of the Church, was a blind poet, and deserves gratitude for having prevented Robert Burns from emigrating in desperation. George Campbell of Aberdeen (1719-1796) wrote very clearly, and made much the best reply to Hume's famous attack on miracles.

Alexander Gerard (1728-1795), Professor of Divinity at Aberdeen, published celebrated Essays on Taste and on Genius. He carefully avoided theological hair-splitting, which he thought the main cause of the increase of unbelief. A contemporary journal wrote of his sermons: "It gave much pleasure to hearers of taste and sensibility to see religion stripped of gloom and arrayed in an elegant, engaging dress." He believed that Patronage served the useful purpose of encouraging independence and culture among ministers.

Alexander Carlyle of Inveresk (1722-1805), the most picturesque of the Moderates, has left us his 'Autobiography,' amongst the most fascinating productions of its kind. "He was one of the noblest looking old gentlemen I almost ever beheld," says Cockburn, and Sir Walter Scott speaks of him in similar terms. On account of his fine appearance he was called 'Jupiter' Carlyle. He was a shrewd man of the world, kindly, and broad-minded, but with a hearty dislike for fanatics.

John Home (1722-1808), minister of Athelstaneford, wrote a tragedy entitled 'Douglas,' which was a great success on the London stage. A Scot who heard it is said to have turned exultantly to an Englishman and exclaimed, "Whaur's your Wullie Shakespere noo?" Evangelical opinion was strongly against the theatre, and raised an outcry against Home, who resigned his charge to avoid serious trouble. Others who attended performances of the play were censured, 'Jupiter' Carlyle amongst them, and the General Assembly of 1757 ruled that ministers ought not to attend the theatre. A change in public opinion is indicated by the fact that in 1785 evening sittings of the General Assembly were adjourned to enable members to hear the great actress, Mrs Siddons.

The Two Parties within the Church.—A very clever and amusing skit upon Moderates was the work of John Witherspoon, an Evangelical minister who became head of Princeton College in America. The faults of the type are easy to discover. We may notice that while they might be expert in History, Philosophy, Literature, or Agriculture, their interest in Theology was slight. They loved the ancient classics and modern literature more than works on Dogma. They laid stress on Toleration and Broad-mindedness rather than on Conviction. They were very much afraid of uncovering the soul or exposing religious feelings. Enthusiasm they despised as vulgar and as showing want of self-control. They admired Reason and Restraint. Their sermons were said to be cold morality rather than warm gospel. They were gentlemen welcome in polite society, and not puritanically rigid. It was felt that they tended to worldliness and carelessness and formality. Some of them had little spiritual life or passion for promoting religion. They included also, however, men of outstanding intellectual ability, solid principle, complete sincerity, and genuine piety.

To the Moderate the Evangelical seemed bigoted and narrow-minded, gloomy and morbid, devoid of a proper sense of proportion, over-emotional and over-excited, inclined to self-righteousness, cant, and uncharitableness. Such were no doubt the possible temptations of that type ; but their virtues were no less in evidence, their over-ruling interest in the eternal, their belief in Revelation, their sense of Providence, their consciousness of human corruption and God's justice and mercy, their devotion to prayer and Bible reading and serious piety, the ardour and pathos and unction of their services, their earnest efforts to face the problems offered by the nature of God and of man, their passion for the saving of souls.

The General Assembly in the second half of the eighteenth century was perhaps more like a Law Court than the centre of the country's spiritual life. Its time was taken up largely with cases and disputes. Its meetings were indeed not without interest. Thomas Somerville (1741-1814), in 'My Own Life and Times,' writes : "The plain good sense expressed with astonishing ease and propriety, which generally marked the speeches at the Bar by ministers from the country, who were not in the habit of taking part otherwise in public business, would have done honour to any assembly or court in the kingdom. Many Lords of Session, advocates, and country gentlemen of rank and opulence, sat as ruling elders on the benches of the General Assembly, and both by their presence and the part they took in its business contributed to the dignity of the court; and some of those Scottish gentlemen who were afterwards most highly distinguished in Parliament first gave promise of eminent capacity for public affairs in the Assembly."

The Assembly had to discuss the growth of dissent, for by 1765 there were said to be a hundred thousand people connected with Burgher, Anti-Burgher, or Relief Churches. In 1777 it was expressing a scarcely moderate indignation at the 'turbulent and ungovernable spirit' of the American rebels. In 1778 there was much agitation throughout the land about the proposal to release Roman Catholics from some of their political and civil disabilities. Robertson and his party took the side of toleration and liberty of conscience; but there was extraordinary popular excitement in the opposite direction and no-popery riots in Edinburgh, Glasgow, and London, and the suggested emancipation was postponed for many years.

Ever since 1736 it had been the custom of the Assembly to make a protest against Patronage as a grievance; but the Moderates had more and more ceased to regard it in that light, and the Assembly of 1784 put an end to this annual practice.

In 1780 Robertson retired from the leadership of the Moderates, and by 1789 there were signs that the influence of the party was declining.

Books to read:—

G. Struthers, 'History of the Relief Church.' (1863.)
A. J. Campbell, 'Two Centuries of the Church of Scotland.' (1930.)
'Autobiography of Alexander Carlyle.' (1910 edition.)
W. L. Mathieson, 'The Awakening of Scotland.' (1910.)

CHAPTER XVI.

THE EVANGELICAL REVIVAL.

Unity in Difference.

"From scenes like these old Scotia's grandeur springs
That makes her lov'd at home, rever'd abroad."

So wrote Robert Burns at the close of his famous description of family worship in the 'Cottar's Saturday Night.' The persistence of such simple faith and reverent religious observance in the latter part of the eighteenth century was due to the Seceders and to the Evangelicals within the Church of Scotland. At the same time Burns reminds us of the want of Christian spirit in those days when still—

"Man's inhumanity to man
Makes countless thousands mourn."

He also reveals how much crude superstition, how much disgusting dissipation, how much hypocrisy, how much lack of spirituality characterised his time. Even the great Communion occasions had for many lost their religious significance. He exposes equally the 'grace-proud' face of the one type and the 'barren-shine' of the other.

All Scots were certainly not of one type. Not even all Presbyterians were alike. The extent to which Presbyterianism in Scotland had been dividing and sub-dividing has often been lamented. 'Schism' is a great sin. James Durham, the seventeenth century Covenanting writer, exhorts Christians to "walk under the impression of the dreadfulness and terribleness of such a plague." Boston reminds us that "it is a great weakness that people cannot value one gift, but they must undervalue another. Many cannot build up one in their esteem, but they must needs have the ruins of others for a foundation."

Want of unity amongst Christians is in the interests of anti-Christian forces. One-sidedness is inevitable. Charity is weakened. The points of difference rather than the main principles of Christianity tend to be emphasised. The breaking up of the Church in Scotland made discipline, education, and the care of the poor more difficult, and led to 'secularising' or the taking over of certain functions by the civil authorities.

On the other hand, if a group separates from the main body, its special message has a better chance to be made clear. Each separation may add to the richness of the total witness. If there are several Churches they inspire one another to greater activity and to a higher standard. Discontent finds an outlet, and more people and kinds of people can have what appeals to them and a position in which they can serve. The highest unity is a unity in difference—a unity that includes the greatest possible variety. Those who separate are generally persons of real conviction, interested, independent, people with ideas, ready to sacrifice for their beliefs; and this is a valuable type.

Changes in Scottish Life and Thought.—As we draw towards the close of the eighteenth century we find one type of Scottish Christianity beginning to strengthen its influence until we can see clearly an Evangelical revival. This change was associated with social and political developments. Scotland was affected by the Industrial Revolution and by the French Revolution. The linen trade, developments with regard to iron, the improvements resulting from the work of James Watt, the Clyde trade in tobacco and cotton, the growth of towns, progress in the matter of transport, somewhat late beginnings of agricultural enterprise, the increase and redistribution of wealth, the appearance of the modern banks, all helped to produce a very different Scotland from that of half a century earlier. People wanted newspapers, clubs, concerts, better houses, tidier streets. In the world of politics and promotion Henry Dundas was omnipotent. As Cockburn says: "It was to his nod that every man owed what he had got and looked for what he wished."

Democratic ideas were stimulated by the happenings in

France in the period from 1789. Robert Burns was much affected by the Revolution, and his "poems and songs are a programme of social and political reform and progress, or at any rate aspiration." Robert Haldane speaks of being "awakened from the sleep of spiritual death" by the French Revolution. Many had high hopes of a better world. World tendencies were really with the Evangelicals. Feeling and philanthropy were uppermost. Wilberforce (1759-1833) was working towards the abolition of the Slave Trade, which he achieved in 1806. The 'Edinburgh Review,' founded in 1802, was on the side of Liberty. It was of those progressive times that Wordsworth wrote :—

> "Bliss was it in that dawn to be alive,
> But to be young was very heaven."

At the same time the Conservatives were made more conservative by the horrors reported from France. The Moderate party had now no great men left. It retained its coldness, but lost its brilliancy. It became more formal and legalistic, less open-minded and common-sense.

Many people were shocked by the infidelity that prevailed amongst the revolutionaries.

> "Reason, philosophy, fiddledum, diddledum,
> Peace and Fraternity, higgledy, piggledy,
> Higgledy, piggledy, fiddledum, diddledum."

French free-thinking seemed the logical result of the ideas upon which the Moderates had been nourished. They began to lose hold, and there was a reaction towards orthodoxy. This tendency may be said to have reached its height in 1831 with the deposition for heresy of a very devout thinker, John Macleod Campbell, minister of Row.

Religious Conditions in Scotland.—We must now look at some of the Evangelical developments. There was more individual and personal religion. In many homes Boston and Ralph Erskine and Willison and Howie's 'Scots Worthies' were being read. Praying Societies flourished. It was under Evangelical stimulus that the Church did something in the way of church extension by setting up Chapels of Ease where the population had greatly increased.

The Evangelicals had advanced with the times. They had broadened in the last half-century. Sir Henry Moncrieff

(1750-1827), one of the ministers of St Cuthbert's, Edinburgh, was among the Evangelical leaders in those days, and Cockburn's account of him gives us a glimpse of the newer fashions in clerical life. We have a picture of how on Sunday he walked to his church "with his bands, his little cocked hat, his tall cane, and his cardinal air; preached, if it was his turn, a sensible, practical sermon; walked home in the same style; took tea about five; spent some hours in his study; at nine had family worship at which he was delighted to see the friends of any of his sons; after which the whole party sat down to the roasted hens, the goblets of wine, and his powerful talk."

An extremely interesting sketch of Church life in the later eighteenth century and early nineteenth will be found in the 'Annals of the Parish' and other novels of John Galt (1779-1839).

The work of the laymen Robert and James Haldane and John Campbell was a feature of the period. Robert Haldane was a naval man and his brother was in the merchant service; Campbell was an Edinburgh ironmonger. They went about preaching, distributing tracts, and starting Sunday Schools. James Haldane wrote: "We consider every Christian is bound, whenever he has opportunity, to warn sinners to flee from the wrath to come, and to point out Jesus as the way, the truth, and the life; whether a man declares these important truths to two or two hundred, he is, in our opinion, a Preacher of the Gospel." The General Assembly of 1799 sent out a Pastoral Letter warning the people against these itinerant and independent evangelists. In the previous year the Anti-Burghers had forbidden their members to hear them. They deposed a minister for doing so. The Relief Synod declared against lay preaching. The evangelists responded by denouncing what they believed to be the defective teaching of the Churches. Modern Scottish Congregationalism began with this mission work. Chapels were built and preachers provided, largely at the expense of the Haldanes. By 1805 they are said to have had some two hundred stations in Scotland. The Haldanes became Baptists, and some of the congregations for which they had been responsible followed them, and this marks what is really the beginning of the present Baptist denomination in Scotland.

Minor controversies of the early nineteenth century must be mentioned in passing as indicating the trend of the times. A contest took place in 1805 between Evangelicals and Moderates over the election to the Chair of Mathematics in Edinburgh University, the former successfully supporting an independent scientist as against an Edinburgh minister, chiefly on the ground that a minister's work required all his time and energy. There was much discussion at this period about Pluralities—that is, the holding of more than one ostensibly full-time position by one man. It was quite common for a professor to hold a ministerial charge along with his Chair, mainly because the University endowments at that time were so small. Thomas Chalmers in his earlier days believed in and practised pluralism. Not till much later did the Church finally come to the conclusion that the practice was bad for the Church, and must cease. It was the Evangelical sense of the seriousness and importance of the work of the ministry that led to this finding. The Napoleonic Wars, the enthusiasm roused by that struggle and the evils that inevitably accompanied and followed it, gave the Church abundance of problems to face and tasks to perform.

Scottish Interest in the Outside World.—Another direction of Evangelical effort at this time was that of Foreign Mission work. The missionary ideal was present to the mind of John Knox, for the title-page of the 'Scots Confession' bears the text, St Matthew xxiv. 14; and the 'Confession' concludes with the prayer, "Let all nations cleave to Thy true knowledge." Samuel Rutherfurd thought much about the conversion of the Jews. The Directory of 1645 teaches prayer "for the propagation of the gospel and kingdom of Christ to all nations." But only when colonising began do the Churches seem to have been roused to any practical interest in this part of their admitted responsibility.

When Scotland sent out the ill-fated Darien Expedition in 1699 ministers were included amongst the colonists and directed to "labour among the natives for their instruction and conversion"; but one of them reported, "Our converse with the Indians, though with dumb signs, is more satisfying than with the most part of our own people. Several of them came to our meetings for worship, and we have exercised in their families when travelling among them, where they behaved themselves very reverently, but we have neither language nor interpreter. But our people do scandalise them, both by stealing from them and teaching them to swear and drink."

The Society for the Propagation of Christian Knowledge, established in 1709, while it confined most of its attention to the Highlands and Islands of Scotland, subscribed money for the salary of David and John Brainerd working among the American Indians. During the later eighteenth century the General Assembly from time to time commended such work abroad.

But modern Foreign Missions are usually dated from the sailing of William Carey for India in 1793. In 1796 the Synods of Fife and Moray overtured the General Assembly in favour of Foreign Missions, but after a lively debate the idea was rejected. The opinion was advanced that heathen nations must be educated before they could appreciate Christian truth. Old Dr Erskine supported the overtures and called attention to St Paul's expression: "I am debtor both to the Greeks and to the barbarians" (Romans i. 14). Carlyle of Inveresk and Dr George Hill, now leader of the Moderates, opposed the proposal. A distinguished lawyer took the view that missionary work encouraged sedition and political unrest. The Anti-Burghers and the Relief Synod both adopted much the same attitude as the majority in the Church of Scotland. The Burgher Synod was more sympathetic.

Unofficial Missionary Societies had been formed in Edinburgh and Glasgow in 1796. Money was raised and missionaries began to be sent out. Peter Greig, who sailed to Sierra Leone in 1797, was murdered a year later by the natives. The work of these Societies at first can scarcely be said to have been very efficient or effective. But a beginning had been made. The London Missionary Society was founded in 1795, and sent out such well-known Scottish missionaries as Robert Morrison, who sailed for China in 1807; Robert Moffat, who went to South Africa in 1816; and, greatest of all, David Livingstone (1813-73), who made his first visit to Africa in 1840. Under one of the Scottish Societies John

Wilson went to India in 1829, and began educational work in Bombay. After the Church of Scotland had officially committed itself to foreign missionary endeavour, Wilson became one of the Church's missionaries, and his enterprise is commemorated in the name of the Wilson College, Bombay. As a result of petition to the Government, Presbyterian chaplains began in 1814 to be appointed for India, an arrangement which long continued. The first of these chaplains was Dr James Bryce, who, after some experience of the country, presented a Memorial to the Assembly of 1824, urging the Church to take up Foreign Mission work. As a result of this and of various overtures from different parts of Scotland, a Committee was appointed to devise "a specific plan." The motion for the appointment of this Committee was proposed by Dr John Inglis (died 1834), minister of Old Greyfriars, Edinburgh, who was at the time the leader of the Moderates. He became the first Convener of the Church of Scotland Foreign Mission Committee.

The first missionary of the Church of Scotland was Alexander Duff (1806-1878). He studied at St Andrews, where he was deeply influenced by Thomas Chalmers, then Professor of Moral Philosophy. Soon after leaving college he was ordained, and sailed with his newly married wife for India. After an adventurous voyage he began educational work at Calcutta, the beginning of the present Scottish Church College. On visits to Scotland he did much by his eloquence for the cause of Missions. "Let us enter," he would say, "into a Solemn League and Covenant before our God in behalf of that benighted land, that we will not rest till the voice of praise and thanksgiving arise in daily orisons from its coral strands, roll over its fertile plains, resound from its smiling valleys, and re-echo from its everlasting hills."

At the Disruption of 1843, Duff, like nearly all of those engaged in work abroad, took the side of the Free Church. His work in India continued until 1863, when he became Convener of the Free Church Foreign Mission Committee at home, and as Professor of Evangelistic Theology gave lectures to the students in the three colleges of the Free Church with a view to inspiring them with new interest in Mission work. He was Moderator of the Free Church in 1873.

Educational work was also achieved by Anderson in Madras

from 1837 and by Hislop at Nagpur from 1844. Other forms of missionary effort were likewise started, and the foundation laid for the extensive missionary work which Scotland carries on in all parts of the non-Christian world.

Books to read :—

W. L. Mathieson, 'Church and Reform in Scotland.' (1916.)
G. Smith, 'Life of Alexander Duff.' (1879.)
T. Johnston, 'The History of the Working Classes in Scotland.'

CHAPTER XVII.

THE VOLUNTARY PRINCIPLE.

The Relation of Church to State.—The question of the relation of Church and State took on a somewhat new complexion as the Secession Churches strengthened. There were now several Churches within the single State, and the problem was the proper attitude of the State to each and all of these. The Church of Scotland had inherited the old connection and the responsibilities and privileges of a National Church. The others had seceded for various reasons from this body or had been begun apart from it, and by reason of the circumstances of their origin had no claim to similar recognition. They had to build churches for themselves, and pay the stipends of the ministers whom they appointed. They enjoyed the feeling of independence which this gave them; but it was only natural that they should sometimes feel annoyed that the ordinary member of the Church of Scotland had fewer burdens to bear. It was also evident that the Church of Scotland could not now claim to be the National Church in the sense of being the Church of the whole nation.

This aspect of things had not occurred to those responsible for the First or the Second Secession; but in 1796 the New Light Burghers made it clear that they had come to the conviction that there should be no State Church, and that governments should not concern themselves with ecclesiastical affairs. This had long been taught by Independents in England.

Thus emerged what was called the Voluntary Principle, and this came to be one of the leading characteristics of the United Presbyterian Church. Voluntaries were right in holding that the Scottish Church had always maintained the doctrine of spiritual freedom; and this they felt was continually in danger if any State connection was admitted, as the State would certainly regard itself as entitled to some return for its support, and so might interfere unduly. But the Voluntaries went further. Personal piety was strong among them, and they held religion to be an individual matter, protesting that those who wished to have a church and a minister should be prepared to pay for them. French Revolution principles fortified the belief in the individual and his rights and responsibilities; and the Reform Act of 1832 was a plain indication of this same democratic tendency in the times. Very similar views regarding religious freedom appeared at this period in other countries—Switzerland, France, Holland, and even Norway—while the experience of the Colonies and of America added encouragement. Among the Scottish Voluntaries the congregational idea was not pressed, and by-and-by strong congregations did assist the weak. Endowments were also accepted, and some United Presbyterian churches drew a considerable income from investments. But the general rule was that congregations should be self-supporting, partly at least on the ground that people incline to value highly what costs them something and to set little store by what is merely given them. Voluntaryism appealed all the more forcibly because economic conditions at the time happened to be such as made it easily possible to provide the money required for ministers and buildings.

According to the Voluntary a congregation is a group of keen and earnest believers. This has sometimes been called the 'sect' view as opposed to the 'church' view. There is the same kind of opposition as showed itself so strongly in seventeenth century France in the famous struggle between the Jansenists and the Jesuits, the former strict, puritanical, zealous, elect, setting a high personal standard; the latter more anxious not to lose hold altogether of the mass of people, however unsaintly, and therefore willing to accept a lower individual standard and a more formal church connection. The 'sect' wants only converted souls. The 'church' since the days of the Emperor Constantine has been more interested in preserving a decent normal. The one is anxious not to admit hastily, the other not to exclude hastily. The first would have the membership of a congregation restricted to such as show some active interest in the cause of the Kingdom; the second feels that only a small proportion of any community is ever zealous about anything, and that it is important that the population as a whole should be kept in some kind of relation with Christianity rather than be driven into opposition. In practice it appears to be difficult to combine these complementary views of the Church.

Spread of Voluntaryism.—Voluntaryism created considerable controversy in Scotland about 1830. The Church of Scotland was coming to recognise that the large towns were under-churched, and that there were districts throughout the country where movements of population had made the provision of Church ordinances insufficient. It was from the legal and practical sides a difficult thing to achieve any alteration on the existing arrangement of parishes; but the Church approached government to have money granted to endow some new churches. The endowments of the old parishes were regarded as in some sense the rightful patrimony or inheritance of the Church, and indeed but a small return for what had been appropriated at the Reformation by government and landowners. This new request, however, was for direct State support. We are now accustomed to the governing authorities supporting from public funds road-building, housing improvements, playing fields, public libraries, and other schemes which benefit some particular section of the people. A small grant had actually been made by Parliament in 1810 for religious work in the Highlands. But Voluntaryism objected to State aid whether direct or indirect, and now successfully opposed any application of public money to the support of a particular religious body; and in spite of the strenuous efforts and oratorical power of Thomas Chalmers new endowments were not forthcoming. Chalmers had consequently to set about raising the necessary money by private subscription. He was no believer in the Voluntary system. "A far more glorious consummation," he said, "is when the State puts forth its hand to sustain and not to subjugate the Church, and the two, bent on moral conquests alone, walk together as fellow-helpers towards the achievement of that great pacific triumph, the Christian education of the people." His exertions at this time increased the number of charges in the Church of Scotland by over two hundred

Voluntaryism received support from the widespread alarm aroused by the Catholic Emancipation Act of 1829. This measure of relief from political disabilities was mainly the result of the efforts of O'Connell in Ireland; and it was feared that the next step might be the establishment of the Roman Church in that country on the ground that it was the majority religion. One means of escape from this possibility was to have no established churches at all; and Dr Marshall of the Secession Church in Kirkintilloch led the way in advocating this.

We may recall the position of Romanism in Scotland. At the Reformation Parliament had suppressed Romanism and proclaimed that there was only one 'face of Kirk' in Scotland, the Reformed Church. A few nobles and lairds retained their old faith, and their tenants followed suit. The Huntly territory and some of the Western Isles were chiefly affected. Although Assemblies and Presbyteries were active in pursuit of all suspects, and although popular dread was very real, as the National Covenant reminds us, the actual number of Romanists was small. The policy of James II. favoured those of his own faith, and this was a principal cause of the Revolution which dethroned him. The attempt to relieve Romanists of certain disabilities in the later eighteenth century gave rise to the Gordon riots in 1779. In that year it was reported to the General Assembly that there were less than 20,000 Romanists in Scotland. By 1829 there were as many as that on the Clyde alone as a result of Irish immigration. The Romanist historian Bellesheim gives a long list of the disabilities of his co-religionists. They amounted at least to very serious discouragement. A Romanist had no political rights, and though the penal statutes were seldom enforced they were always there. Priests were not supposed to be allowed in the country at all. The Catholic Emancipation Act introduced toleration at last. In 1878 the hierarchy was restored in Scotland, archbishops and bishops being appointed. Recent times have witnessed the phenomenal growth of the number of people in Glasgow district who are of Irish extraction. These have all the privileges of citizenship, and indeed the

Education Act of 1918 gives Romanism in some respects a favoured position.

To return to the Voluntary Principle. Occasion was found for asserting the principle in connection with the Edinburgh Annuity Tax. In early times burghs had naturally provided churches and ministers. No one thought of any other way in which they could have been provided. Often appropriated Church property or accumulated teinds were employed for this purpose. In the nineteenth century, though many people did not any longer attend these churches or accept the services of the ministers, the obligation to maintain them remained. In Edinburgh the required funds were obtained from what was practically direct taxation, and members of the Secession churches objected to pay. Dr John Brown of Broughton Place Church was one of those who refused in 1838. The annuity tax was finally abolished in 1870.

The United Presbyterian Church.—In 1820 most of the Burghers and Anti-Burghers had come together in Bristo Church, Edinburgh, to form the United Secession Church. With this body the Relief Church combined in 1847 in the Tanfield Hall, Edinburgh, to constitute amidst great excitement the United Presbyterian Church. Professor MacEwen writes: "The Union was a natural if not an enthusiastic one. Its influence upon both Churches was in all respects beneficial, resulting not only in greater corporate strength, but in the removal of tendencies which had limited the work of each when separate." There were 518 congregations in the new denomination, including those in England, and before many years it could claim 160,000 in attendance at its services.

The United Presbyterian Church was marked by evangelical character, self-sacrificing liberality, and democratic spirit. It was somewhat broader in its outlook than the early Seceders had been, and was independent as being self-governing and self-supporting. Its members were in close sympathy with the Liberal party in politics; and took an active interest in promoting social reform, the abolition of slavery, the cause of temperance, the removal of religious tests for university professors (1852), and latterly, though without success, the disestablishment of the Church of Scotland. Any intolerant or persecuting doctrine which might be found in the Westminster Confession was explicitly disowned.

The United Presbyterian Church was proud of its Divinity Hall. In the days of the First Secession there had been only one professor, and the students had to gather at his Manse in Perth, or Abernethy, or Whitburn, or wherever the professor's charge might be. The United Secession Church in 1825 instituted a second Chair, and in 1834 the number was increased to four. The students were numerous. They received an intensive training during a two months' session for five years after the completion of a University Arts Course. For a time certain classes met in Glasgow and others in Edinburgh. The students of the Relief Church until 1824 attended the University Divinity Halls. Some time after the United Presbyterian Church was formed the teaching was concentrated in a Theological Hall in Edinburgh, and an extended course provided.

Some distinguished figures amongst United Presbyterian ministers may be mentioned.

John Brown of Broughton Place (1784-1858), son and grandson of well-known Seceding ministers of the same name, a passionate and energetic and rousing preacher, a pastor who proved what a pastor could be, well-read in biblical theology, the author of numerous biblical studies, and the forerunner of more liberal theology and discerning exegesis, was one of the authoritative, compelling personalities of his day. A description of him says: "His face was beautifully chiselled, almost like marble; his forehead was high and bare; his thin white locks flowed lengthily over his ears and collar; his eye was black and piercing like an eagle's—it seemed as if it were looking you through; his voice was clear and ringing, sometimes trumpet-like."

Perhaps the best known of all was John Cairns (1826-1892). He was reared in a Border shepherd's cottage, was of massive build and strong physique, great intellectual capacity, deep spirituality, simple character, and gracious manner. He ministered for many years at Berwick. A member of his congregation said of him: "Ay, I suppose he was a fine preacher, but I know that he was my kind, dear friend." His biographer describes how "he stood up among the worshippers, not only as a prophet, but as a priest who bore them on his heart before God continually." In 1869 he was appointed Professor of Apologetics at Edinburgh, and in

1879 he became Principal of the Theological Hall. His publications were few and his lectures unequal, his expression never seeming to be adequate to his powers, but his personality excited veneration and trust. One utterance shows his point of view: "We cannot compress too much work for Christ into one short life."

John Eadie (1810-1876), who combined a busy pastorate in Glasgow with the Professorship of Biblical Literature from 1843, was an able scholar, with a well-stored mind and a ready wit, was amongst the first to appreciate German biblical studies, and himself published many volumes helpful to the Bible reader. He had a share in the production of the Revised Version of the English Bible which began in 1870. We hear of his "herculean build and Jove-like head," "his fair mane of hair in such profusion."

Among preachers foremost place is by common consent assigned to Dr John Ker (1819-1886). The United Presbyterian Church created for him the Chair of Practical Training in its Edinburgh Theological Hall. He was an orator of distinction, and in spite of broken health exerted powerful influence. Dr Blaikie writes of his sermons: "They draw from the harp of Grace a softer music . . . than most fingers have been able to evoke."

The Life and Work of the Church.—The United Presbyterian Church gave full scope to popular opinion and to lay activity. Its Synod, or highest governing body, was not, like the Assemblies of the Church of Scotland and the Free Church, a representative body, but included all ministers and an elder from every congregation. It was democratic, and insisted upon having freedom to appoint Moderators and officials and professors and committees without previous arrangement. The laity had more authority and the minister less independence than in some other Churches. The minister had no standing as far as the management of finance was concerned: all such matters were in the hands of trustees or managers, frequently well-to-do business men. The Church was especially strong in Glasgow, where many men who had made good in the city liberally supported it. Another district where the Church flourished was the Orkneys, where a sadly neglected field was discovered.

The Church was aggressive in foreign missionary work, the

Calabar Mission in Africa, led by Hope Waddell, being its particular interest in the early days. It was to this field that Mary Slessor (1848-1915), the Dundee mill-girl, went out in 1876 to begin her romantic career. Under the United Presbyterian Church, Dugald Christie of Mukden was a distinguished medical pioneer in Manchuria, while at Livingstonia in Africa, Robert Laws (1851-1934) became the best known of the devoted missionaries.

The United Presbyterian Church showed itself progressive in the matter of the singing of hymns. There was some increase of fervour and enthusiasm as a result of the famous revival which spread from America to Ireland and Scotland in 1859. In the sphere of theology, the United Presbyterian Church, under the guidance of Principal John Cairns, led the way in Scotland in declaring for liberty of thought on any matters "not entering into the substance of the Faith"; and also registered its abandonment of certain of the sterner doctrines of Calvinism as expounded in the Westminster Confession. Theological differences had occurred, and James Morison of Kilmarnock was deposed by the United Secession Church in 1841; and his views found expression in the Evangelical Union Church which ultimately joined with the Congregationalists. At a later date several other cases produced a consciousness that while general adherence to the Westminster Confession must be required, there must also be room for liberty of thinking within this limit. A common position would seem to have been that of Dr John Brown of Broughton Place, which was defined by his son in these terms: "The doctrines of Calvin, mitigated but not renounced, and received simply as dictates of heaven, without any effort or hope to bridge over their inscrutable depths by philosophical theories, he translated into a fervent, humble, and resolutely active life." Compare this with the teaching in the 'Catechism' by James Fisher, one of the Secession leaders. The advance marked by the Declaratory Act of 1879 may be claimed as one result of the independence of the United Presbyterian Church.

A Wider Union.—Negotiations for union with the Free Church commenced in 1863. Dr John Cairns strongly supported the movement, and it met with no opposition in the United Presbyterian Church. In the other body the situation was different, and the idea of union was dropped in 1873. It was once more with practical unanimity that the United Presbyterian Church made the first move towards reopening this possibility in 1896, and with similar heartiness it entered into the Union when at last achieved in 1900 by the formation of the United Free Church.

Books to read :—

J. Cairns, 'Life of John Brown, D.D.' (1860.)
A. R. MacEwen, 'Life and Letters of John Cairns.' (1895.)
D. Woodside, 'The Soul of a Scottish Church.'

CHAPTER XVIII.

THE DISRUPTION.

The Disruption of 1843 has been described as "the most honourable fact for Scotland that its whole history supplies." When it was announced that more than 400 ministers had 'gone out,' Lord Jeffrey expressed a widespread opinion when he declared: "I'm proud of my country. There is not another country upon earth where such a deed could have been done."

The Veto Act.—How then did this notable event in Scottish history come about? In 1832, the year in which democracy triumphed with its Reform Act, a motion was introduced in the General Assembly to make the people's share in the election of ministers a reality by insisting that the 'call' was not merely an expression of good will after a presentation, but a document essential to a legal induction. The 'call' is a signed document addressed by a congregation to a minister-elect inviting him to accept the pastoral charge offered him and promising co-operation. The motion was defeated by the Moderate majority in the Assembly, and a similar fate met a motion put forward by Thomas Chalmers in the following year to the effect that "the majority of dissentient voices should lay a veto on every presentation." Veto literally means "I forbid." But the Evangelical party had been growing in strength, and after this date proved supreme in the Courts of the Church.

At the 1834 Assembly Lord Moncrieff, a Scottish Judge, moved again for the power of veto, taking the line that this would only mean the restoration to practice of what had always been the law of the Church of Scotland. He argued that the Patronage Act of 1712, while it gave back to patrons the right to present ministers, proposed no change in the manner in which a presentation must take effect through the people's 'call' and through Presbyterial examination and induction. The leader of the opposition on this occasion, Professor Duncan Mearns of King's College, Aberdeen, a clear-headed debater, pointed out that the Veto Bill involved innovation in giving the last word to congregations, the Scottish practice having been that the Courts of the Church had the last word. The Veto Act was, however, carried by a substantial majority, was sent down to Presbyteries, approved by a majority of these, and became the law of the Church at the Assembly of 1835. The principle of the Act was stated in these terms: "It is a fundamental law of this Church that no pastor shall be intruded on any congregation contrary to the will of the people." From this expression the Evangelicals became known as the Non-Intrusionists.

It should be observed that the Veto Act was proposed by a lawyer, but that the lawyers in the Assembly were not agreed among themselves as to what the Church could or could not legally do in the way of making such an Act. The opponents were of opinion that as such a law affected the rights of patrons, rights which rested upon State enactments, the Church in passing it was interfering in the sphere of the State. It was also pointed out that while the 'call' had been an expression of positive support, the Veto Act introduced something new in assigning legal importance to the negative side and the objections offered.

The Chapel Act.—This energetic Assembly of 1834 also accepted the Chapel Act, which in due course became the law of the Church next year. Districts had been assigned to certain new churches or chapels, and this Act proposed that all such churches should have the same status as the old parish churches in matters *quoad sacra* (or affecting religion), that they should accordingly have Kirk Sessions of their own, and that their ministers should have seats in the Courts of the Church. These new churches were a result of Evangelical activity, and the congregations and ministers generally belonged to the Evangelical party. The Act would thus incidentally increase the proportion of Evangelicals in Presbyteries and Assemblies and bring the party more power. This was a point which naturally occurred to the Moderates.

The Evangelicals were anxious to encourage the new churches and thus to give an impetus to the setting up of many more similar charges instead of leaving people to join the Secession churches, where they would at once have full rights accorded them. But it was the legal question that was most pressing.

Dr R. J. Brown, Professor of Greek at Marischal College, Aberdeen, who proposed the Chapel Act, assumed that it was within the power of the Church to legislate on this matter. Dr George Cook, Professor of Moral Philosophy at St Andrews, held, on the other hand, that the State had provided certain ways of erecting parishes, and whatever views one might have on that matter, it was not for the Church to make other laws to suit itself, but to take steps to have the existing law altered constitutionally through Parliament. Presbyteries had responsibility in connection with various civil matters, in relation to presentations to parishes, to stipend payments, to school affairs. Was it within the power of the Church to make a law which would alter the membership of a court dealing with these civil questions ? It was the difficult problem as to where the line must be drawn between the functions of Church and of State.

Local Disputes.—A vacancy at Auchterarder was the means of bringing the conflict of Church and State to a head. In 1834 Robert Young, a man of respectable character and duly qualified, but a poor preacher and lame, was presented to the parish. Only three persons signed the 'call' while 287 recorded their veto against him. The objections were not all to the presentee. Many were anxious to take this first opportunity of using their rights under the new Veto Act, and to express hostility to a presentation of any kind. On appeal the matter came before the General Assembly, and that body, in accordance with the Act, instructed the Presbytery to reject Mr Young. The patron and the presentee thereupon raised a civil action in the Court of Session on the ground that, the presentation having been duly made, the Courts of the Church had no choice but to examine the selected minister, and, if he were found spiritually and intellectually qualified, to admit him to the parish. The point at issue was really whether the Veto Act was legal or whether in enacting it the Church had gone beyond its powers. In the Law Courts in 1838 eight Judges gave their opinion for the State and five for the Church. The law of the land was thus pronounced to be that if a man were chosen by a patron neither congregation nor any Court of the Church could hinder his induction, so long as he had the ordinary moral and educational qualifications. The Veto Act was declared contrary to the constitution of the Church of Scotland. This decision was a serious blow to the freedom of the Church and to the hopes of the democratic party.

The most celebrated case of all, and the one which caused most bitterness, was that of Marnoch, in the Presbytery of Strathbogie. It became so involved that people spoke of the "reel of Bogie." A vacancy occurred in 1837, and the patron presented Mr Edwards, then assistant in the parish. He was not without accomplishments, but had made himself unpopular. and only four signed the 'call,' while 261 recorded their veto. In accordance with the Veto Act the Assembly of 1838 ordered the Presbytery to reject the presentee, and the Presbytery obeyed. The patron then proposed a Mr Henry; but Mr Edwards applied for an interdict to prevent Mr Henry's induction, and raised an action to compel the Presbytery to proceed with his own trials. The Strathbogie Presbytery by a majority now resolved that "the Court of Session, having authority in matters relating to the induction of ministers and having interdicted all proceedings on the part of the Presbytery, and it being the duty of the Presbytery to submit to their authority regularly interposed, the Presbytery do delay all procedure until the matter in dispute be legally determined." They held that whatever one thought of the law it must be obeyed until it could be constitutionally altered. The minority held that this was sheer Erastianism.

The Commission of Assembly (the Committee to which an Assembly delegates certain of its functions for the interval between the annual Assemblies) censured the Presbytery of Strathbogie and prohibited the induction. The Court of Session declared that the Presbytery was legally bound to take Mr Edwards on trials with a view to inducting him. Which authority was to be obeyed? The majority of the Presbytery decided that the law of the land was the final judge, sustained the call to Mr Edwards, appointed his trials and reported the whole matter to the Commission. The Commission suspended the majority of the Presbytery and instructed the Evangelical minority of four to carry on the work of the Presbytery. The majority appealed on legal grounds, but the next Assembly upheld the decision of the Commission. Meantime, the majority acted as if not suspended, celebrated Communion, and held Session meetings. They now obtained an interdict from the Court of Session to prevent the minority from coming into their parishes; but the minority made a special point of entering those parishes and holding public meetings there, and the Court of Session did not press the interdict against them. In the meanwhile, Mr Edwards had passed his trials before the Strathbogie majority and secured a decision of the Court of Session that he was entitled to be inducted to Marnoch. The majority accordingly inducted him against the orders of the General Assembly and against the wishes of the people. A great concourse of interested onlookers watched as the members of the congregation, having entered their protest, solemnly and dramatically abandoned the church of their fathers. In consequence of this day's work the Strathbogie majority were deposed from the ministry by the Assembly of 1841.

Crisis in the Church.—An entirely intolerable situation plainly existed in Scotland. Obviously Church and State required to come to some understanding. Possibly a satisfactory solution might have been reached and the Church left intact; but the obstacles in the way were enormous. Feeling between the two parties within the Church of Scotland had become intensely bitter. The political situation was also unhelpful. Any measure suggested to Parliament by one political party was strenuously opposed by the other. No agreed plan was possible. Further, the Prime Minister (Lord Melbourne) did not like Dr Chalmers, who was the most prominent of the Non-Intrusionists.

It must, besides, be carefully remembered that England was in this same period faced with the problem of Church and State in a form of its own, and English politicians and churchmen could not but look at the Scottish problem in the light of what was happening nearer home. It was the time of the Oxford Movement. This influential Movement, associated with the names of Keble, Newman, and Pusey, began in 1833 as a declaration of spiritual independence directed against Erastianism and State interference. It permanently affected every part of English church life, involving a spiritual revival, a return to doctrine, a rebirth of ritual, and it developed into the Anglo-Catholicism which to-day remains so restless under the State control to which the Church of England is subject. The leaders of the Oxford Movement and of Scottish Non-Intrusionism held essentially the same view of the nature of the Church and of its relation to the State. People in England who were alarmed at the tendencies revealed by the Oxford Movement naturally proved suspicious of the high claims of the Scottish Evangelicals.

Several Parliamentary efforts were made so to alter the law as to restore ecclesiastical peace in Scotland. Lord Aberdeen's proposals in 1840 were followed by an attempt on the part of the Duke of Argyll and that by a scheme of Sir George Sinclair; but no one was satisfied. Sinclair's Bill would have allowed a Presbytery to reject a presentee if opposed for stated reasons, even if those reasons did not seem to them very convincing. But Dr Candlish, for the Non-Intrusionists, was determined that a 'mere aversion' on the part of the majority of a congregation should be sufficient to prevent an individual's appointment as minister.

Forty Evangelical ministers in the Synod of Glasgow and Ayr declared themselves prepared to accept Sinclair's plan. Their leader was Leishman of Govan. They had sympathisers in other parts of the country, but the group of forty was prominent, and as this third party declined to go out with the rest of the Evangelicals at the Disruption, their Non-Intrusionist brethren dubbed them "the Forty Thieves."

The final effort at settlement was a Bill by Mr Campbell of Monzie, M.P. for Argyllshire, in 1842, which had in the end to be abandoned because of a technical objection on the part of the Government. Sir Robert Peel was now Prime Minister and definitely unfavourable to the Non-Intrusion party. The most prominently hostile of the Cabinet Ministers was Sir James Graham.

The Claim of Right.—The Evangelical majority at the Assembly of 1842 was strong and determined. Dr William Cunningham carried a motion demanding the abolition of Patronage as "the main cause of the difficulties in which the Church is at present involved." There was also passed the celebrated Claim of Right, mainly the work of an enthusiastic layman, Mr Alexander Murray Dunlop. He was a devoted, pious, and disinterested churchman, and played a foremost part in the formation and upbuilding of the Free Church.

The Claim of Right was a lengthy document, insisting upon Christ's headship of the Church, and the spiritual freedom of the Church, declaring that this had always been the claim of the Church, that it had been admitted in repeated Acts of Parliament, that the Church's privileges were guaranteed at the Union of 1707, that the Patronage Act of 1712 was a violation of the Act of Security which was a condition of the Union, that Parliament was now encroaching upon the sphere of jurisdiction of the Church, and that to this the Church was determined not to submit, holding that all Acts affecting the government and discipline of the Church, but passed without its consent, were null and void.

This impressive document would have pleased Andrew Melville, Samuel Rutherfurd, and James Renwick. It was a strong expression of a view that had supporters amongst Scottish Protestants in all periods. Such doctrine, however, had never satisfied all Scotland. It was thought by the Moderates to be fanatical, and bound to produce not a Church for the nation, but a Church for the few. In the Middle Ages Church meant clergy, and State meant laity; and in later times Moderate opinion continued to regard the State as public commonsense capable of putting a check on clerical extremism and making for toleration. Evangelicals did not feel the need of this safeguard, since the Calvinistic Reformation had given lay opinion its opportunity of self-expression within the Church through the place in Church-government assigned to laymen.

The Moderates believed that in a dispute as to whether a matter belonged to the sphere of the Church or to that of the State, the final decision must lie with the State, the law of the land being the fundamental condition of the existence of society. Evangelical opinion was more true to the spirit of Augustine; and inclined to identify the Church with the "City of God," and the State with the "City of the World," the State being thus an unfortunate necessity due to human depravity with the function of making the Church's life and work possible and protecting its liberties.

The Non-Intrusion party were now so powerful and so

fully organised that they decided to abandon the appeal to Government and take matters into their own hands. A meeting of Evangelical ministers was held in November 1842 in the Roxburgh Chapel in Edinburgh. The proceedings were in private. Some 465 ministers were present. They were unanimous as to the existence of grievances arising from the existing relations with the State; and the great majority pledged themselves to secession unless the State agreed to the Claim of Right. There was by this time no serious expectation that the State would so agree, and Dr Chalmers expounded his plans for the possible formation of a Church free from any connection with the State. The motto which he gave his supporters was "Organize, organize, organize."

In the interval trouble had been accentuated in connection with the working of the Chapel Act of 1834. The Stewarton congregation of the Original Secession Synod in 1839 decided to return to the Church of Scotland, and a district was assigned it as a parish and the minister recognised as a member of Presbytery in accordance with the Act. But the heritors obtained an interdict on any alteration of the former parish boundaries, and the Court of Session in 1843 declared that the Chapel Act, like the Veto Act, had been *ultra vires* or beyond the right of the Church to pass. According to this decision the proceedings of Presbyteries which included Chapel ministers were invalid. Parish boundaries could only be altered by the civil authorities.

Both the House of Lords and the House of Commons debated the Scottish situation in the spring of 1843; but the prevailing opinion was that the majority in the Church of Scotland were demanding irresponsible powers, and that in any constitutional country the State must have the last word.

The Parting of the Ways.—Matters came to a head as was anticipated at the Assembly of 1843. The Evangelicals and their families and friends crowded to Edinburgh and public excitement had not been greater since the days of the National Covenant. The Assembly met in St Andrew's Church in George Street, Dr Welsh, the retiring Moderator, presiding. At once the Protest was read, the Disruption of the Church from the State was declared, and Chalmers, Candlish, Cunningham, and other Non-Intrusionist leaders rose and left the Assembly, followed by a long line of supporters. Eventually some 474 ministers out of the 1203, and about a third of the whole membership of the Church, seceded and formed themselves into the Free Church of Scotland.

The procession of ministers and elders marched through a throng of the admiring and the interested to the Tanfield Hall in Canonmills, which had been prepared for the purpose. There, amidst tremendous enthusiasm, the Free Church was founded, Dr Chalmers becoming its first Moderator; and a "deed of demission" was signed and sent to the Church of Scotland Assembly, the ministers surrendering their parishes, manses, and stipends.

The Disruption did not settle the problem of Church and State for Scotland, but it gave dramatic expression to one view of it. It called forth a spirit of self-sacrifice, of loyalty to principle, and of determination to uphold "the Crown Rights of the Redeemer." A most regrettable amount of bitterness was introduced into Scottish life by this Ten Years' Conflict. On the other hand, there can be no doubt as to the spiritual stimulus which it supplied, not only to those who went out, but also to those who stayed in. And into the reunited Church of Scotland of 1929 the Free Church brought all the spiritual freedom it went out to gain.

Books to read :—

W. Hanna, 'Memoirs of Thomas Chalmers.' (1878 edition.)
T. Brown, 'Annals of the Disruption.' (1892 edition.)
R. Buchanan, 'Ten Years' Conflict.' (1849.)
G. D. Henderson, 'Heritage: a study of the Disruption.' (1943.)

CHAPTER XIX.

SPIRITUAL INDEPENDENCE.

Thomas Chalmers.—The hero of the Disruption was Thomas Chalmers. He was born in 1780 at Anstruther in Fife, where his father was a merchant. As a student at St Andrews he developed a taste for mathematics and science; and as minister of Kilmany he was still mainly absorbed in these intellectual interests, his little country parish occupying but a corner of his mind and heart. An illness in 1809 helped to induce concern for spiritual things. Chalmers had great natural eloquence, not seriously hampered by his broad Scots and his Fife accent. Called to the Tron Church in Glasgow in 1816 he was from the first a success as a preacher and lecturer. J. G. Lockhart declared that "most unquestionably I have never heard, whether in England or in Scotland or in any other country, any preacher whose eloquence is capable of producing an effect so strong and irresistible as his." When he preached in London he attained "unrivalled and unbounded popularity." "The tartan beats us all," was the comment of the statesman Canning.

Chalmers took most seriously the pastoral oversight of his crowded city parish, doing house-to-house visitation, organising local Sunday Schools, ordaining more and younger elders than was usual, and in the new parish of St John's to which he removed in 1819 trying out his scheme for proving that the poor could be better cared for under a voluntary charitable system than under a compulsory State assessment.

In 1823 he became Professor of Moral Philosophy at St Andrews, and five years later was elected to the Chair of Divinity in Edinburgh University, where he exerted a profound influence upon generations of students. Impressed by the "gigantic evil" of the unevangelised masses, he threw himself into the task of Church extension, and was the means of erecting in the course of seven years more than two hundred churches, at a cost of over £300,000. As champion of the Evangelical party, he did much to create the enthusiasm necessary for the Disruption; and his foresight and organizing ability contributed greatly to the successful upbuilding of the Free Church and to the soundness of its finances. He died in his sleep in 1847, having been since 1843 Principal and Professor of Divinity in the Church's College in Edinburgh.

Chalmers was not a man of great culture or breadth, but intelligent, sincere, and humble, able to hold the affection even of opponents, passionately enthusiastic, actuated by strong benevolence. His numerous published works are marked by passages of glowing eloquence, somewhat grandiloquent, stimulating rather than exact. He was conservative in ethics and theology as in politics, and it was his personality rather than any originality of thought or expression that counted. "There is something altogether remarkable about that man," said Lord Jeffrey.

Other Disruption Leaders.—In some ways the real leader of the Disruption movement was R. S. Candlish (1806-1873). In his appearance the high and wide forehead was striking, but other features were small, and the whole figure tended to the fragile. At an early age he was called to be minister of St George's, Edinburgh, and his preaching, expository, sympathetic, orthodox, attracted widespread admiration. Only in 1839 did he make his first speech in the General Assembly, but he was quickly in the front rank of the Evangelical party, and took a particularly energetic part in preparing for and guiding the Convocation of 1842 and in planning the steps taken thereafter.

For intellectual grasp, intuitive power of deciding what course of action was expedient, dexterous debating skill, expert managing of men, he was outstanding. Of sensitive nature, somewhat impetuous and impatient, intensely emotional, he was not always in agreement with other leaders; but the Church at large trusted his wisdom, and those nearest him knew his deep affection. Candlish was Principal of the College in Edinburgh from 1862 and in the forefront of all the general activities of the Free Church.

Another of the great debaters was William Cunningham (1805-1861), Professor of Church History and, in succession to Chalmers, Principal of the College, a tall, strong figure crowned with its mop of curly hair, his mind substantially furnished with scholastic learning, skilful and clear in controversy, vehement and crushing in argument, sagacious and sincere, somewhat ponderous and stern, rather lacking in imagination, but a doughty protagonist of Evangelical liberty.

Amongst the 'Disruption Worthies' must also be remembered Thomas Guthrie, preacher and philanthropist (1803-1873); Horatius Bonar, author of many precious hymns (1808-1889); Alexander Murray Dunlop, hero of the Claim of Right (1798-1870); and Hugh Miller, the Cromarty mason (died 1856), whom all the world knows as the writer of 'My Schools and Schoolmasters,' and whose sledge-hammer journalism proved invaluable to the Evangelical party.

Maintaining the New Church.—There can be no doubt of "the peculiar glow, the moral elevation and exhilaration of the years which succeeded the Disruption." Heroic leaders and deeply stirred followers overcame all difficulties. The first months were months of tremendous exertion as well as of tremendous enthusiasm. The Sustentation Fund which Chalmers had devised was wonderfully successful. He was a sanguine schemer, and before the Disruption had given such a glowing account of the plan for providing ministers' stipends in the proposed Free Church that someone said the lifeboat seemed better than the ship. Though the fund did not reach the figure at which he aimed, it was a remarkable achievement. There had been time to prepare carefully, and ministers and people had warning of what the situation was likely to be when the State connection was abandoned. The principle of an equal dividend, the strong helping the weak, was found to appeal better than any of the others proposed.

In two years no fewer than 500 churches were built. They were naturally of the simplest architecture and most of them cost only a few hundred pounds.. It was not an artistic period, and the minds of the Free Church people were on other matters. The first was a brick church in Edinburgh built for Candlish's followers in his St George's congregation in anticipation of the Disruption, and used on the first Sunday thereafter.

Members of the Church were generous to the point of sacrifice, and money was also contributed from America and other homes of freedom. Materials and labour were frequently given free.

Moving scenes occurred as ministers preached for the last time in their accustomed pulpits, or as the minister's wife and children left the Manse which had been their home. There was something of the glorying of martyrdom, but there was also its discomfort. During the summer months many congregations worshipped out of doors. Barns, sheds, disused buildings of all sorts were requisitioned temporarily. There was the famous floating church at Strontian. In some districts landowners refused sites to the Free Church, and this was a source of hardship until finally Parliament interfered in the name of toleration.

A special Manse Fund was raised under the Convenership of Dr Guthrie. Then came the question of schools. Schoolmasters who had joined the Free Church were dismissed by the Church of Scotland authorities who had formerly employed them, but money was raised for Free Church schools to rival the parish schools; and Free Church Normal Colleges followed for the training of a new generation of teachers. The education of candidates for the ministry had to be taken in hand. A college in Edinburgh was started under Dr Chalmers, and by-and-by developed into the splendidly equipped New College on the Mound. It was only after considerable controversy that the Free Church agreed to have colleges also in Glasgow (now Trinity College) and Aberdeen (now Christ's College).

The Expansion of the Church.—The Free Church had no thought of any change in Creed, or Church government, or forms of Worship. Nor had it any need to think out a policy with regard to schemes. Foreign Mission work had in recent times become an important interest of the Scottish Evangelical; and the missionaries had naturally been of this party and consequently adhered to the Free Church at the Disruption. The six missionaries to the Jews did likewise. The Free Church took its full share in such work, in various parts of India and of Africa, in Southern Arabia and elsewhere. Great names include those of Miller of Madras, Stewart of Lovedale, Ion Keith-Falconer. Activity in the Foreign and Jewish fields rapidly expanded, as did also work in the Colonies and on the Continent, until the Church found itself responsible for a vast enterprise abroad such as could only be maintained by the steady zeal of the whole membership of a strong and aggressive religious community.

Church extension was pursued, notably in Glasgow and Edinburgh and in the Highlands and Islands. The congregational life throughout the land was on a high spiritual level, as might be expected among people familiar with their Bibles, earnest in private and family prayer, scrupulously observant of the 'Sabbath,' strictly puritan in conduct, and proud of kinship with the Covenanters. Youth work was always a strong feature. Towards the close of the century Bible Classes were extraordinarily popular, and Dr Alexander Whyte of Free St George's, Edinburgh (1836-1921), was something of a pioneer with his Handbooks for Bible Classes. Evangelical revivals in 1859 and under Moody and Sankey in 1874 influenced a wide circle, and mention must also be made of Henry Drummond (died 1897), who in a wonderful way roused a new religious and social consciousness amongst Scottish students.

In the Free Church elders were elected by the people, and seriously undertook the spiritual oversight of the congregation to the great assistance of the minister, conducting Sunday Schools and prayer meetings, visiting the sick and praying with them, and exercising a kindly and solemnising authority. There were besides in certain Highland areas those remarkable characters called "The Men," deeply experienced Christians conspicuous for theological interest, scripture exposition, and the practice of righteousness.

Development of Religious Thought in the Free Church.—Someone speaking of the Free Church in 1897 said: "She is not going to moor the ship in the harbour of 1843 in which Chalmers and the 400 embarked: she is sailing out into the open to be led where the Spirit listeth." This reveals both the gain and the risk of the freedom won. The Free Church felt itself at liberty to change; but how was it to be prevented from changing in dangerous directions?

One department in which this difficulty arose was that of Bible study. The Scottish Church at the Reformation had turned to the Bible as its standard in all matters of belief and practice. The seventeenth and eighteenth centuries had interpreted scripture very literally, unconscious of many problems involved, and had followed Calvin in drawing little distinction between different parts of the Bible. But the development idea in the philosophy of the German Hegel (died 1831), the theory of Evolution propounded by the English scientist Darwin (died 1882), and the works of Thomas Carlyle (died 1881), one of Scotland's most stimulating writers, were evidence of a new attitude of mind. Both in Germany and in England scholars had begun to study the Bible in the light of such recent thought; and one of the first to do so in Scotland was the brilliant and versatile William Robertson Smith (died 1894), elected Professor of Old Testament in the Free Church College at Aberdeen in 1870 at the unusually early age of twenty-four. An article on the Bible came from his pen in 1875, and caused great alarm in a Church which had so far adhered strictly to the old traditions with regard to Scripture composition, authorship, and authenticity. The Professor was put on trial for his opinions, and the celebrated case occupied Church Courts till 1881, when it was decided that it was not "safe or advantageous for the Church" that he should teach its students. He was deprived of his Chair, but his general position soon came to be widely adopted under the influence of such scholars as T. M. Lindsay, Professor of Church History in the Glasgow College (died 1914), A. B. Bruce, who taught New Testament at the same centre (died 1899), and Marcus Dods (died 1909), who became Professor of New Testament and ultimately Principal in Edinburgh. A commonsense view of the Bible has now largely replaced the former superstitious attitude. Higher criticism in the words of Robertson Smith "means the fair and honest looking at the Bible as a historical record, and the effort everywhere to reach the real meaning and historical setting. . . . This process can be dangerous to faith only when it is begun without faith."

Theological and Biblical study flourished more and more in the colleges of the Free Church, and several of the teachers came to be well known in other parts of the world through their published writings. Opinion on doctrinal matters had undergone a considerable modification since 1843, and a

Declaratory Act was accordingly passed in 1892, permitting diversity of opinion on such points in the Westminster Confession as "do not enter into the substance of the Reformed Faith." There was much opposition to this step, especially from the Highlands, and a small section of the traditionalist minority seceded and formed the Free Presbyterian Church.

Church Union.—Another department in which change of outlook was to assert itself had to do with Voluntaryism. Chalmers was no Voluntary. "We quit a vitiated Establishment," he said, "and would rejoice in returning to a pure one." But in practice Free Church people were Voluntaries, and very effective ones. Thus they developed closer sympathy with the position of the United Presbyterian Church.

Proposals for union between the Free Church and the United Presbyterian Church were put forward in 1863; but to the great disappointment of many, including Dr Candlish, it proved impossible to overcome the opposition strenuously offered by Dr James Begg of Newington, Edinburgh (1808-1883), and a considerable following, many of them from the Highlands; and the scheme had to be abandoned in 1873. Begg had been a popular and energetic minister in a number of charges, and was noted for independence of outlook. His position was nearer to that of the Church of Scotland than to that of the United Presbyterian Church. The most outstanding of his supporters in the North was Dr John Kennedy of Dingwall (1819-1884), who had succeeded to the influence of Dr John Macdonald of Ferintosh, "the Apostle of the North" (died 1849). Kennedy was a preacher of power, a much trusted adviser, a highly respected authority. He took the view that the union movement was "the first fungus growth on the tree planted in 1843." Later, we find him opposing the introduction of hymns and of instrumental music, critical views of the Bible, and the use of railways on Sunday.

The Free Church was as hostile as the United Presbyterian Church to the action of the Church of Scotland in discarding Patronage in 1874, and co-operated with the United Presbyterian Church in the Disestablishment campaigns which terminated unsuccessfully in 1895. This common antagonism to the Church of Scotland helped to bring these two Evangelical churches to a better understanding of one another. Negotiations with a view to an incorporating union were accordingly resumed under the leadership of Dr Rainy in 1897 in response to a definite invitation of the United Presbyterian Church Synod of 1896. Terms were rapidly adjusted, and when finally Presbyteries were consulted the United Presbyterian Church proved unanimously favourable, and in the Free Church only four Presbyteries disapproved.

The United Free Church thus came triumphantly into being in October 1900, Dr Rainy, its first Moderator, expressing his faith that out of that Union would come "a larger Presbyterianism for Scotland, devoted to the advancement of our Lord's kingdom, very friendly, I hope, to the civil authority, very serviceable to the welfare of the nation, but free from the temptations of a statutory connection with the State."

Another statement made by Rainy on that memorable occasion may be quoted: "That the Church of Christ is to be bound for ever to particular utterances put forth by excellent men fifty or sixty years ago—is monstrous. The only authentic Free Church tradition is the right of the Church to determine its own constitution, its own principles, its own doctrine."

This was exactly what the opponents of the Union denied. They held that the Free Church had unlawfully abandoned its Disruption principles with regard to Establishment and with regard to the Confession of Faith. In consequence, they raised an action in the Court of Session to have themselves declared to be the legal Free Church, and to be therefore entitled to all the properties and funds of that Church. A famous trial followed. In 1901 the Scottish Judge in the Outer House of the Court of Session gave his verdict for those who had entered the Union; and on appeal this judgment was unanimously sustained by the three Judges in the Inner House. The case, however, was further appealed to the highest Court in the British Isles, the House of Lords. Here a different attitude prevailed, and in 1904 by five votes to two the Judges gave a verdict for those who opposed the Union, the main point in the view of the majority being that the case was a matter of the law of trusts, and that the Free

Church by joining with the United Presbyterian Church had lost its identity with the Church of the Disruption.

The decision threatened to be a most serious affair for the newly united body; but it was soon obvious that it could not be carried into effect owing to the small numbers in the continuing Free Church, and the very large properties involved. Government consequently stepped in, and made a reasonable allocation between those who were now part of the United Free Church and those who stood out of the Union and survive to-day as the Free Church.

Principal Rainy.—The undoubted leader of the Free Church throughout the last quarter of the nineteenth century and up to his death in 1906 was Robert Rainy. Born in 1826, son of a medical professor in Glasgow, he began his Divinity studies amidst the enthusiasm of the Disruption, and after a short ministry at Huntly, was called to the High Church, Edinburgh, succeeding Cunningham in 1861 as Professor of Church History, and being appointed Principal in 1874.

He became pre-eminently the Church statesman, and after his death his work was well described in the House of Commons by Sir Henry Campbell-Bannerman, the Prime Minister, when he said: "If ever there was a man who was calculated by tact, by ingenuity, by straightforwardness of character, by high talents, and by patriotic motives, to deserve the name of statesman, it was the late Principal Rainy."

He took a prominent part in the great debates in connection with the negotiations for Church Union in 1863-1873, opposing those who were inclined to regard everything about the Disruption as peculiarly sacred and inviolable, and declaring: "The Church of Christ has no liberty to become the slave even of its own history." Later he appeared as champion of the Evangelical view of Scottish history against the Moderate picture given by Dean Stanley (1872); was active against the Patronage Act of the Church of Scotland; guided the Free Church to sacrifice Robertson Smith in the interests alike of peace and of liberty; was in the thick of the Disestablishment campaigns; and was the maker of the Union of 1900 and the sagacious upholder of the Church in the crisis of the House of Lords case. A progressive, if perhaps opportunist leader, a skilled diplomatist, of striking figure, severe of countenance, reserved in manner, of indomitable faith, a man of vision, he was regarded with intense dislike by such as found themselves in opposition to him, but with boundless admiration by the Church in all whose troubles and triumphs he so fully shared.

Books to read :—

N. L. Walker, 'Chapters from the History of the Free Church of Scotland.' (1895.)
P. Carnegie Simpson, 'Life of Principal Rainy.' (1909.)
G. F. Barbour, 'Life of Alexander Whyte.' (1923.)
H. Watt, 'Thomas Chalmers and the Disruption.' (1943.)

CHAPTER XX.

THE NATIONAL CHURCH REVIVES.

The Recovery of the Church.—The Church of Scotland, after the painful impairment which it had undergone at the Disruption, experienced a slow convalescence and for a time walked but feebly. In the long run it not only recovered, but was in some ways better and stronger for what had happened. It is true that most of the zealous both amongst ministers and amongst members had gone out. It is also true that many of those who remained did so out of mere lethargy; it is easier to do nothing than to do something. At the same time many remained in the Church of Scotland on principle, when it would have been easier to allow themselves to have been swept out on the wave-crest of enthusiasm and emotionalism, and when they could easily have earned popularity by so doing. To some the movement appeared hysterical and fanatical. It seemed to them that a little patience would have remedied all that required remedy. And they frankly disliked the extremer Evangelical type.

Congregations in many parts of the country followed the example of their minister, and either stayed in or went out as he did. In some places, on the other hand, an Evangelical congregation took the opportunity to escape from an uncongenial ministry. The degree to which the parish churches were affected varied very much in different parts of the land, some districts declaring solidly for the Free Church and others quite as solidly for the Church of Scotland. In many places the congregation simply split in two.

The opinion of Thomas Erskine of Linlathen (1788-1870), a layman whom Chalmers called "a holy, spiritual, enlightened, and affectionate Christian," may be quoted. "I doubt not that a certain kind and degree of good may arise amongst certain persons out of our Scottish kirk separation—more awakened thought, more zeal—but I fear also more judging, more spiritual pride, &c., as in the much and perhaps over-lauded days of the Covenant. . . ." "The great body of the people here have followed Mr Miller out of the Church rather (I believe) on the ground that he is a good man and making a sacrifice for conscience's sake, than on any personal convictions of their own that the principle on which he acts is right. I believe also that it is generally felt that the rights of the people are asserted by the seceding minister, which weighs a good deal."

It was necessary to do what was possible towards filling the many vacancies. No Church could suddenly produce fit men for so many places. The situation was similar to that of the Church of Scotland at the Reformation before the required number of men could be adequately trained as ministers. In 1662 the Episcopalians had the task of finding several hundred 'curates' to take the place of the 'outed' Covenanters; and after the Revolution Settlement in 1690 the Presbyterians in their turn had to fill numerous pulpits from which Jacobites had been ejected. In all these cases men might be employed who were not of the highest standard, spiritually, morally, or mentally. After 1843 some ministers were promoted to charges more responsible than they had dreamt of seeking, and men who had previously failed to be elected to any parish now found themselves in demand. Though there were actually 500 probationers available, most of them in teaching posts, there were difficulties, and even the Free Church had to ordain some who had not yet finished their college course. Through time this rectified itself, and there was no lack until recent years of suitable candidates for the ministry.

The Church of Scotland was assisted in its recovery by the fact that its machinery may be said to have been unaffected. Its church buildings, manses, and stipends remained as before in every parish. It retained its prestige as the National Church, and had old associations which meant a great deal to people. Some perhaps preferred it because it did not press for money, but others liked it for its calm and breadth and sanity. Time has proved that it had not lost the regard of the people and that the country needed it.

The Church of Scotland was also stimulated by the new sense of rivalry, and even by the bitter attacks to which it was subjected by such writers as Hugh Miller, who demanded that the parish minister be treated "as the one excommunicated man of the district, the man with whom no one is to join in prayer, whose church is to be avoided as an impure and unholy place." In later periods the existence of the other Presbyterian churches was a constant incentive. The separate denominations kept one another awake to the opportunities and wants of the moment. There was considerable ill-feeling at times and very little intercourse, but each found work to do and each made its contribution to the life of the community.

The Church of Scotland soon had to be relieved of the duty of caring for the poor, a burden which it had long and honourably borne; and presently it found its responsibility for education also less heavy, since it was now shared with the Free Church.

Church Extension.—After the Disruption the Church of Scotland went back to the position which it had occupied before the Veto Act and the Chapel Act. There was, not unnaturally, a conservative period, when Dr George Cook, deep in Church law, survivor of the old Moderates, set the tone. Presently, however, a new spirit asserted itself. Perhaps this showed most clearly in the work of Church extension. It was felt that "an established Church . . . fails to fulfil its mission if all possible efforts are not made by it, effectually to provide for the spiritual destitution especially of the poorer classes of society." Energetic measures were taken "that the Gospel should be zealously and efficiently preached in localities and among people whose spiritual welfare, if it has not been hitherto neglected, has at least been but imperfectly cared for." By 1860 sixty new parishes had been erected and money raised sufficient to provide a guaranteed endowment for each of them. Fifty years after the Disruption the Church of Scotland had added 400 such *quoad sacra* parishes to its numbers.

The impetus for this important achievement came mainly from Dr Robertson, who had been interested in the cause under the influence of Chalmers. James Robertson (1803-1860) was brought up on an Aberdeenshire farm, entered Aberdeen University at the age of twelve and distinguished himself there in mathematics, became headmaster of Robert Gordon's Hospital, a residential school for boys in Aberdeen, and in 1832 was appointed minister of Ellon, whence he removed in 1844 to be Professor of Church History in Edinburgh University. A man of unwearying diligence, "an agonising worker," devoted to his duty as a parish minister, of deep convictions and in deadly earnest about whatever he undertook, not brilliant, not eloquent, inclined to exhaustive trains of thought in his sermons and speeches, but clear-headed in debate, warm-hearted, and able to infect others with his enthusiasms, he wore himself out in the service of the Endowment Scheme.

In 1873 Robertson's intimate friend, James Baird of Cambusdoon, made over to the Church a gift of £500,000 towards this kind of work. The Baird Trust is still an active agent in connection with evangelical effort within the Church of Scotland.

Fresh Advances.—The same period saw the Church released from that control of the election of ministers by patrons which had been one of the main causes of Secession since it was reimposed by the British Parliament in 1712. Democratic ideas had gained ground very widely in the past half-century. The second Reform Act of 1867, with its extension of the franchise, showed the direction of public opinion. The Education Act of 1872 marked a new stage in the process of fitting the individual citizen to take an intelligent interest in public affairs. The new *quoad sacra* parishes under the Endowment Scheme had brought popular election into the practice of the Church of Scotland. In all the circumstances Patronage was doomed. The Act of Parliament abolishing it was passed in 1874 and brought the Church of Scotland into line with the Free Church and the United Presbyterian Church in this matter, and into accord with the general trend of public conviction.

The work of the Church in connection with Foreign Missions saw steady expansion. A fresh field had been opened in the Punjab in 1855, but the missionary and his wife and child were killed in the Indian Mutiny (1857). Interest in the people of India, however, increased after the Mutiny, and new efforts resulted, perhaps the most dramatic development being the sending of J. A. Graham to Kalimpong in 1889 under the auspices of the Young Men's Guild whose first Secretary he had been. The cause of African missions received great impetus in Scotland from the popular sympathy roused by the achievements and death of David Livingstone, and the Church of Scotland in 1876 commenced work at Blantyre, where a magnificent church now bears witness to the success of the effort. In China a beginning of missionary endeavour was made in 1878 at Ichang. Mission work, evangelical, medical, and industrial, by an increasing number of men and women, has gradually asserted itself as a normal activity of the Church and one of its most honourable obligations. The greatly extended and deepened knowledge now at our disposal with regard to other races and their conditions, and the feeling of world unity due to modern facilities for travel, have encouraged missionary zeal.

The Church of Scotland also persevered with work among the Jews, and in the Colonies ; and the number of its schemes and committees increased with the growing complexity of modern problems.

Education for the Ministry.—The Universities in Scotland, as elsewhere, had always been closely connected with the Church. It was the Pope who gave the necessary permission for the foundation of a university. The main purpose was to provide an educated clergy, and the institutions were naturally under the careful supervision of the ecclesiastical authorities. Before the Reformation education had not been neglected in Scotland. The country had several universities and a number of flourishing grammar schools, and Scottish students were familiar at foreign seats of learning. A famous Act of 1496—which unfortunately did not have much effect —required the eldest sons of noblemen to have 'perfect Latin' and some knowledge of law. The Reformation, and particularly the Calvinistic Reformation, made new intellectual demands on the people. They were expected to study Bible and Catechism and to follow the sermon. For this education was required. Knox would have liked to see a school in every parish, and though money for the purpose was not available and it was not until the eighteenth century that the attainment of this ideal can be said to have been approached, the Church was still the one body which interested itself in the matter. The universities likewise constituted a particular concern of the Church and remained under its control. Principals and professors were normally ministers of the Church of Scotland and certainly always members. Difficulties began when the Church of Scotland ceased to be the only lawful Church in the land. The Disruption brought matters to a head. The sectarian divisions in Scotland opened the door for the secularising (or taking over by the civil authorities) of the universities, as also of the care of the poor, the infirm, registration, and the schools. Not merely the Church of Scotland, but the Church at large lost its hold. It became clear that one denomination could not be allowed a monopoly in university teaching; and the result was that by Act of Parliament in 1852 all the Chairs (except those in Theological subjects) were freed from religious tests and so made open to persons of any or no religion. At the Church Union of 1929 it was further arranged to untest certain Theological Chairs, and this policy has since been carried further.

The Disestablishment Movement.—Towards the close of the nineteenth century the Church of Scotland was very seriously attacked with a view to its disestablishment and disendowment. In order to defend its position the Church in 1882 appointed a Church Interests Committee which was nobly served by such leaders as Lord Balfour of Burleigh and Mr Christopher Johnston (later Lord Sands), and after very exciting campaigns the Church emerged in 1895 unscathed and all the stronger for the marvellous evidences of true affection which the danger elicited from its members.

Changes in Worship.—Within the Church one of the most interesting movements was that associated with the name of Dr Robert Lee of Old Greyfriars, Edinburgh (1804-1868). He had been a particularly brilliant student at St Andrews University, and throughout his career showed a capacity to think for himself even when it meant standing alone against general opinion. He was a man of culture and taste, strong-minded and courageous, precise and critical. His outstanding contribution to Scottish Church life was in the province of Worship, where he was the pioneer of 'order and decency.' He advocated the use of organs and the improvement of Church music, urged that ministers should carefully compose prayers and read them in church rather than trust to whatever might come to them at the moment, that worshippers should kneel in prayer, and that 'responses' by the congregation should be encouraged so as to hold attention and give an active share in the devotions. Lee maintained that he was in all respects true to the teaching of the Reformers and to the Directory for the Public Worship of God (1645), and he deplored the slovenliness which he found common in Scottish Church worship. Much opposition was roused by his practices, and the Church as a whole has not accepted his views in detail; but there can be no doubt that he called attention to a real defect, and that he contributed largely to bring about marked improvement in the externals of public worship. The discussion of these matters at the time served a useful purpose in making clear the policy of the Church, that much freedom may be allowed to ministers and congregations with regard to anything not fundamental; but that nothing should be attempted that is likely to create dispeace throughout the Church or seriously to strain feelings of good-will within a congregation.

Under the influence of Professor William Milligan, a greatly beloved teacher at Aberdeen (1821-1893), the Scottish Church Society (1892) helped to awaken zeal for the old paths. A similar direction of interest and activity characterised the career of Professor James Cooper (1846-1922). During a remarkable ministry in the East Church of St Nicholas in Aberdeen, and afterwards as occupant of the Chair of Church History in Glasgow, he stood valiantly for closer adherence to the ancient Christian Church in doctrine and worship. He inspired many with a profound sense of the sacredness and responsibility of the work of the ministry, and was the founder of the Scottish Ecclesiological Society which has done much to improve taste in matters of church building and furnishing. He encouraged the study of the old liturgies and a revival of emphasis on the sacramental teaching of the Church.

Leaders of the Church.—For some considerable time the trusted leader of the Church was its Principal Clerk of Assembly, John Tulloch, Principal of St Mary's College, St Andrews (1823-1886). A son of the manse, he was educated at St Andrews and Edinburgh, and described at that stage as "slim, fair, tall, and mirth-loving." From his skilful pen came a succession of works, chiefly dealing with historical theology and religious biography, showing a deep reverence for the past combined with lively faith in progress. A power in the university life of Scotland, an acceptable public speaker, a sagacious administrator, a favourite with Queen Victoria, he was a man of sound intellect, broad sympathies, liberal outlook, and impartial judgment.

Amongst many whose names are still honoured may be mentioned: John Caird (1820-1898), Principal of Glasgow University, distinguished for the clear thinking and powerful utterance of his sermons; George Matheson of Innellan (1842-1906), the blind author of the hymn, "O love that wilt not let me go"; A. K. H. Boyd of St Andrews (1825-1899), one of the most famous of anecdotists; Robert Flint of Edinburgh (1834-1910), a theologian of world-wide repute.

No figure is more attractive than that of Norman Macleod of the Barony Church, Glasgow (1812-1872). His ancestors lived in the island of Skye. His grandfather and father were ministers of Gaelic-speaking charges; his tall uncle John was named "the high priest of Morven"; his cousins, Norman of Inverness and John of Govan, made their mark in the Church. After a thoroughly Highland childhood, a student's training at Glasgow and Edinburgh, and an impressive sojourn on the Continent, he became minister at Loudon, then at Dalkeith, and finally in the great city parish of which his name is the chief pride. Macleod was a man of wide sympathies, his ministry as much a source of blessing to crowds of working-class men and women as it was to the Queen at Balmoral. He strongly believed that the function of the Church was not only the conversion of sinners and the edification of saints, but the advancement of "all that pertains to the well-being of the community." His pastoral and parochial work was outstanding, for he worked hard, his nature was friendly, he had a sense of humour, his personality was inspiring, he had a genius for organising, and he was not tied down to traditional methods, but had something of the pioneer spirit. As a preacher he was natural and conversational, growing passionate and moving, and giving his packed congregations of eager listeners confidence that he understood them and that what he said came from the heart and was true. The Disruption movement had not attracted him, though he admired Chalmers. He was a broad-minded man, opposed to narrow puritan ideas about the Sunday and many other matters. 'Good Words,' a healthy and instructive popular magazine which he edited for many years, met a real need at the time and had a wide circulation. His writings, such as 'The Old Lieutenant and His Son,' 'The Starling,' 'Reminiscences of a Highland Parish,' provided edifying reading much appreciated by ordinary Church-loving people. Perhaps Norman Macleod's ideals are summed up best in his own words: "I desire to be broad as the charity of Almighty God. . . . I desire to be narrow as God's righteousness, which, as a sharp sword, can separate between eternal right and eternal wrong."

It must at the same time be kept in mind that the life and health and progress of the Church does not depend upon a few distinguished personalities. The unobtrusive labours of countless unknown warriors in the work of the ministry in town and country, the thousands of true believers and faithful practising Christians in all classes of our community, elders, Sunday School teachers, deaconesses, choir members, and so many other valuable types, are in great measure responsible for the continuance of the Church as a spiritual force from one generation to another.

Books to read :—

J. R. Fleming, 'The Church of Scotland, 1843-1929.' (1927, 1933.)
J. Cunningham, 'Church History of Scotland.' (1882 edition.)
A. H. Charteris, 'Life of James Robertson.' (1863.)
'Memoirs of Norman Macleod.' (1876.)

CHAPTER XXI.

A CENTURY OF CHANGE.

Changing Ways.—There is often cause to remark how averse people are from changes in religious matters. They like the practices to which they have been accustomed, though they may not know anything about their origin; and they resent any attempt at innovation. Habit plays an important part in the ordinary person's life. And a sense of proportion is sometimes not very highly developed.

It must, however, be pointed out that a tradition fixes itself more quickly than is frequently noticed. Many seem to imagine that the ways to which they have themselves been used in Church have always existed, everywhere exist, and are necessary. Yet customs which it might be difficult to persuade people to give up may not be more than a generation or two in age, and may be common only within a limited circle.

At the same time, changes do slowly and steadily and imperceptibly take place; and one cannot study the nineteenth century without being particularly impressed by the many and great differences that may be traced between the Scottish Church at the close of that century and the Scottish Church a few generations earlier. There can be no question that the Church has in a remarkable manner shown its power of adaptation. Though it is naturally somewhat conservative, it has never ceased to recognise its duty of meeting the special needs of each age as well as those fundamental needs of the human soul which are the same in every century.

In a peculiar degree the nineteenth century was characterised by change. We note the flood-tide of Democracy, and the extension of the right to vote; the appearance of the Trade

Union, Socialism, Co-operative Societies; the development of the railway and steamboat; the invention of telegraph and telephone; the tremendous growth of the large towns, with the necessary improvements in lighting, water supply, police, and municipal government; the rise of imperialism to its climax and the steady increase of Free Trade prosperity; unprecedented industrial and commercial enterprise; the spread of the ability to read and the consequent supply of newspapers and popular literature; marvellous advances in science, medicine, surgery, and general knowledge; the emergence of new social problems and new ruling ideas, such as that of Evolution. The keynote of the period was progress; and the twentieth century has continued the process at an even swifter and more revolutionary pace.

The Scotland of the nineteenth century was closely linked with England; and while in literature it supplied Byron and Scott and Carlyle and R. L. Stevenson, it accepted Wordsworth, Tennyson, and Browning as if they were its own. In the world of Religion the two countries were in much the same position with regard to the new attractions of German philosophy and theology, the conflict between Science and Religion and the modern approach to the Bible.

Changes in the National Life.—The Church in Scotland affected and was affected by all the processes of change that were at work.

The Kirk Session remained, as it still remains, a prominent feature of congregational organisation, but its functions underwent serious alteration. An important part of the elder's duty in earlier periods had been the care of the poor. But in 1845 the State took over this responsibility. The voluntary system of poor relief with its helpful personal contacts became impracticable through the development of city populations, the number of dependants left by the Napoleonic struggle, the loss both of parish control, and of financial resources which the Secessions and the Disruption involved for the Kirk Session, as well as new conceptions of the rights of citizens and the duty of the community; and it was necessary that provision for the poor should become a matter for the civil authorities with their power of taxation.

Another regular function of the Session had been the supervision of education. The relation between Church and school had been close. Ministers and elders had much say in the appointment of teachers, and these had to accept the Westminster Confession and were often men who had at least begun a course of study for the ministry, who made a special feature of instruction in Scripture and Catechism, and who guided the cleverest boys to think of some day occupying a pulpit.

There was, however, no means whereby the Church could obtain the money necessary for providing a thoroughly adequate education system in a period which was convinced at last that education was part of the proper equipment of every individual. The Church, as in so many departments, had done the pioneering work and satisfied the people as to the value of education; and in 1872 the whole matter passed into the hands of the civil authorities, and a new scheme for the schooling of every child was inaugurated.

For some time ministers and elders as members of school boards retained their influence, but Acts of 1918 and 1929 have reduced this considerably. Religious instruction is given by the regular school teachers on lines agreeable to the Churches. This does not, however, include the teaching of the distinctive features of this or that denomination. Roman Catholics and Episcopalians continue to have Church schools with denominational teaching by clergymen, while at the same time these schools are maintained by national taxation.

Colleges for the training of teachers were controlled by the Churches until 1906, and until recently the Church of Scotland provided the Directors of Religious Education in the training centres. The whole question of religious instruction is of the first importance for the Church, and there are some difficult problems connected with it. Its place in secondary schools may be mentioned as one of these.

Another considerable change in the work of the Kirk Session was the gradual abandonment of the traditional Church discipline. The existence of a number of denominations side by side took away the control which the session once had over every inhabitant of the parish. Sessions ceased to take their former interest in the precise manner in which parishioners observed the Lord's Day. Charges of witchcraft and charming had disappeared. The stool of repentance, sackcloth, and the jougs had fallen out of use. Public appearances for moral offences have been rare since 1840; and such matters are now generally dealt with privately by the minister. Excommunication became practically unknown.

Changes in Worship.—Changes have taken place in connection with worship. They did not come into evidence everywhere at the same time. As a dwelling or a spinning-wheel may still be found in Lewis of the same style as prevailed there some hundreds of years ago, so religious customs long abandoned in certain parts of Scotland continue to be observed in others. In a Church of Scotland congregation in the Hebrides it may be that the minister will wear no gown; there will be no instrumental music; the precentor will chant each line of the psalm before leading the singing of it; no hymns will be permitted; the people will stand for prayer; and the Sunday will be kept with scrupulous strictness. But generally speaking, methods have altered enormously, and most of all in the large towns.

The 'lecture' was still common in the Disruption period; but it died out, and the straightforward reading of Scripture was restored. The Church of Scotland Assembly in 1812 recommended ministers to read a passage of the Bible at one of the Sunday services; but only in 1856 was this made a definite instruction. There is occasional mention of choirs in the eighteenth century and early nineteenth century; but in most places it was not before the second half of the century that these began to appear in the seat below the pulpit, which the elders had been wont to use. Paraphrases were allowed in some Churches from the time of their first appearance in 1781, and hymns were known in the Relief Church before the end of the eighteenth century; but again it was not till the second half of the nineteenth that the singing of hymns was taken up seriously, and hymn-books produced leading to the present Revised Church Hymnary of 1927.

The Scottish Church had followed Calvin in his disapproval of organs. The first attempt to introduce an organ was at St Andrew's Church, Glasgow, in 1804; but it was not till Dr Robert Lee had boldly raised the question in 1863 that the Church of Scotland began to change its general attitude in this matter. The U.P. Church soon followed; and in

1883 the Free Church, in spite of strenuous and influential opposition, permitted the use of instrumental music. Since then the musical side of public worship has enormously improved. It was Dr Lee who was mainly responsible for the greater care and orderliness that have come to characterise Scottish religious worship. He insisted that the Church in Scotland, chiefly in the conflict with Episcopacy and under English puritan and independent influences, had departed from the type of worship which approved itself to Knox and to the first Covenanters. Some have since gone very far in the direction of ritual and ceremonial; but the general taste seems still to be for a simple service. The practice of extemporaneous or free prayer finds continued approval; but there has been improvement with regard to both the form and the content of public prayers. Ministers have given time to the study of prayer language and to the prayer utterances of great souls. It is felt that the Holy Spirit will use effectively the prepared rather than the vacant mind and heart. And it is realised that a congregation will join most easily and profitably in following an ordered prayer, and will be helped if invocation, thanksgiving, confession, supplication, and intercession can be clearly distinguished. The more liturgical prayers are formal frameworks into whose familiar and very general phrases the worshipper fits his own personal needs. Free prayer is already personal and individual, and while it is therefore sometimes difficult to make it the channel for the prayers of many types of worshippers at once, it is valued for its peculiar warmth and emotional strength.

The sermon retained that central position in the service to which Calvin, with his high regard for reason and his low opinion of the senses, had raised it. People were expected to have a reason for the faith that was in them and so must be instructed. The preacher had the holy office of a prophet of the Word of God. Sermons were still expository, doctrinal, and practical, with a Moderate emphasis on conduct or an Evangelical plea to close with Christ. But the sermons gradually shortened from an hour and more to twenty minutes, and an attempt was made to have them interesting rather than exhaustive. The style (like that of the speeches in the House of Commons) became greatly simplified. The popular contempt for anyone who 'read' his sermon slowly vanished. Even the minister's black gloves have quite disappeared, though they survived into the twentieth century. Popular lectures upon what were termed semi-religious subjects came into fashion and went out of it again. A higher standard of expectation manifested itself with regard to sermons as congregations became better educated and more widely informed, and as people began to go to Church rather because they wanted to go than because it was the custom. The tendency of the most recent period is to depend upon experts in all departments of life and thought—the specialist in surgery, the permanent official in government, the leader writer in politics; and so it would appear that people now once again look to preachers to speak with authority.

Communion continued to be celebrated in most congregations no more than twice or four times in the year. The idea of corporate Communion rather than individual Communion has remained uppermost in Scotland. The service began in the nineteenth century to be observed simultaneously in the ordinary pews instead of in groups at a Communion Table specially set up in the church. Only the use of white cloths on the pews keeps alive the old suggestion of a supper table. With the abandonment of the 'tables' came the more general introduction of a small permanent Communion Table where the sacred vessels were placed on Communion Sunday. In many places there has been a revival of emphasis upon the sacraments, and the Communion Table has been given something of the position and importance of an altar. The Communion token gave place to the printed card; the Fast Day disappeared; the Tent preaching ceased; and in many churches the individual cup was introduced; and the question of unfermented wine was raised.

In the matter of church architecture there were great advances in the latter part of the century. It is a happy change to find many churches open all the week for private prayer and meditation. Some return is being made to the religious observance of Christmas and Easter. Churches were not heated or lighted in earlier days; but with modern developments in such matters greater comfort was attained. Evening services became possible, and soon popular.

Church Organisations.—A new step is marked by the

introduction of halls in connection with churches. This was associated with one of the revolutionary changes in church life in the later nineteenth century, the beginning of the numerous 'organisations,' a development due to the emergence of the group or community spirit which is recognised as a special feature of our era. Former generations were content with a weekly prayer meeting and perhaps a choir practice. But Sunday Schools, which had been in the earlier decades of the century mostly small groups of children privately gathered by pious ladies or elders, acquired new importance as more attention came to be paid to the young and to their education, and as the Church lost control of religious instruction in day schools. Bible Classes for adolescents supplemented this work and fitted young members of the Church for young communicants' classes. The Boys' Brigade was founded in 1883, and other uniformed organisations more or less closely associated with, though not controlled by, the Church, have proved helpful. The Woman's Guild of the Church of Scotland was founded in 1887 by Professor A. H. Charteris of Edinburgh (1835-1908), and in recent times has become, both socially and spiritually, a most valuable institution in nearly every congregation. A beginning was made with whole-time service for women as Church sisters. Social life also came to be cultivated to a new degree, and societies of many kinds were started in connection with congregations. The difficulty has sometimes been so to guide these as really to advance the spiritual well-being of those interested. Organisations may do much to foster Christian life; but, on the other hand, it is possible for them to be mere parasites on the Church. All the organisations are under the minister and Kirk Session; and the supervision of them has become one of their most serious responsibilities. In speaking of organisations we may lay stress upon the extensive and active interest which the Church has learned to take in the welfare of youth. We may also note the increasing importance of the part played by women in the work of the Church.

Theological Outlook.—The century witnessed gradual broadening in theological outlook. Eighteenth-century theology in Scotland tended to be "dull, Dutch, and prolix"; but influences from England and Germany introduced new life. Schleiermacher and Hegel made a deep impression. English Broad Church leaders, such as F. D. Maurice (died 1872) and Charles Kingsley (died 1875), also found followers. The volume of 'Scotch Sermons' published in 1880 was one indication of a tendency to leave the old paths of scholastic Calvinism. The U.P. Church was the first to relax the formula to be signed by ministers at ordination (1879). This was followed by the Free Church (1892), and ultimately by the Church of Scotland (1905), so that now, instead of accepting the letter of every article of the Westminster Confession, a candidate for the ministry is required to state no more than that he believes "the fundamental doctrines of the Christian faith contained in the Confession of Faith of this Church." New Biblical critical ideas were introduced and gradually overcame first suspicions. The foundations were laid for a more scientific study of history. Butler's 'Analogy' and Paley's 'Evidences,' which had abundantly satisfied mid-century apologists, had fifty years later completely lost their reputation. Recent tendencies in belief may be judged from the almost complete disappearance of the Shorter Catechism in day school and Sunday School and from the 'Short Statement of the Church's Faith,' issued in 1935 by the reunited Church of Scotland. A new Catechism is projected.

The nineteenth century saw the beginnings of the increasingly rapid change which has taken place in the general attitude to Lord's Day observance. Dr Norman Macleod strongly insisted upon the distinction between the Jewish Sabbath and the Christian Sunday. And the present-day outlook has the virtue of being partly a result of our liberation by science from fear and superstition. The modern Christian is, however, more and more threatened with the complete loss of his Holy Day, and the situation is one which can only be observed with alarm.

Books to read :—

D. C. Somervell, 'English Thought in the Nineteenth Century.' (1929.)
G. D. Henderson, 'The Scottish Ruling Elder.' Chapter VII.
E. Haldane, 'The Scotland of our Fathers.' (1933.)

CHAPTER XXII.

THE REUNITED CHURCH OF SCOTLAND.

The Essential Unity of the Church.—The Church of Scotland claims to be part of the "One, Holy, Catholic, and Apostolic Church"; and in so doing shows the importance it attaches to the unity and continuity of Christianity. Psalm 133 is a favourite: "Behold, how good and pleasant it is for brethren to dwell together in unity." A famous early Christian document is St Cyprian's tract on 'The Unity of the Church.' The Lausanne Conference of many denominations on "Faith and Order" in 1927 unanimously agreed that "God wills unity. . . . However we may justify the beginnings of disunion, we lament its continuance, and henceforth must labour, in patience and faith to build up our broken walls."

Presbyterianism, according to a distinguished writer, Matthew Arnold, "is born to separation as the sparks fly upward." The many divisions and differences whose occurrence we have noted offer some ground for the criticism, and the Union movements of the nineteenth and twentieth centuries were in part due to a sense of guilt in all concerned. It should, however, be observed that the division of opinion within Presbyterianism never involved the fundamentals of the Faith, and was always evidence of real earnestness about religion.

Protestantism from the beginning encouraged people to think for themselves. And wherever men are thinking, some variety is inevitable, and within limits is felt to be rather a good thing. We must also distinguish between unity and uniformity. In the seventeenth century uniformity or sameness of belief and practice was what all parties desired. But there can be unity amidst differences. Science reminds us that the higher organisms show more variety than the lower. There are greater differences amongst human beings than amongst moles or frogs. Our Lord's Apostles were far from being all alike in spirit, character, or ability. We recognise as Christians persons so diverse as St Francis of Assisi, St Teresa, John Calvin, Archbishop Laud, John Bunyan, John Wesley, General Booth, Cardinal Newman. Gregory the Great reminded his clergy that in any congregation there were many contrasting types of people all requiring to be dealt with in differing ways. And in an age of specialisation like ours, the variety is still more evident and important.

Calvin laid much stress upon the 'invisible' Church; and this made it less urgent to insist on unity in the 'visible' Church. The main thing is unity of Spirit. A visible unity, however, is possible in spite of much diversity. The duty of attempting to achieve visible union was emphasised in the seventeenth century by the Scot, John Durie, who travelled extensively in Europe preaching unity. The great philosopher Leibniz (1646-1716) was an eager advocate of the same cause. And in Scotland in the nineteenth century an impulse was given to the movement by the Unions of 1820 and 1847, by the entry into the Free Church of most of the small Original Secession Church (1852) and Reformed Presbyterian Church (1876), by the blending of Congregationalism and the Evangelical Union (1897), and by the successful merging of the United Presbyterian and the Free Churches in 1900. That the tendency is not merely provincial is proved by recent unions of Churches in Canada (1925), among the English Methodists (1933), amongst the French Protestants (1938), and in the attempt at an even broader union in South India (1947).

Movement Towards Corporate Unity.—The Church of Scotland Assembly in 1869 had before it an overture on the subject of Presbyterian Union, and in the following year accepted a motion declaring "hearty willingness and desire to take all possible steps consistent with the principles on which the Church was founded to promote the reunion of Churches having a common origin, adhering to the same Confession of Faith and the same system of government and worship." But there was still strong hostility amongst

Presbyterians in Scotland, and parties sought to produce uniformity by overcoming and crushing others, rather than to attain unity by a more tolerant and comprehensive plan. The fierce Disestablishment campaigns organised by Free churchmen and United Presbyterians against the Church of Scotland were in the interests of religious equality by conquest. They failed for political reasons in 1886 and again in 1895. But this was the last attempt to settle matters by war methods.

Many things helped the cause of Union. The Union of 1900 had proved a success; and it was evident that if the Free Church and the United Presbyterian Church, with their very different traditions, could unite, there was nothing impossible about the thought of a wider union. The size of the newly formed United Free Church had the effect of leaving the Church of Scotland with a diminished claim to be the National Church. The Church of Scotland had for some time been actually engaged in the work of Church extension, and there were now hundreds of *quoad sacra* charges existing upon what was practically a voluntary basis.

The problem of the relation of Church and State had greatly altered. The very content of the words 'Church' and 'State' had changed considerably. The attitude taken by government in 1843 was now unthinkable. Of recent years the State had not shown itself at all an enemy to a progressive Church. The State had acquiesced in the abolition of that patronage which it had itself insisted upon in 1712; and in 1905 it had agreed to such a relaxation of the formula to be signed by ministers at Ordination as made the Church the interpreter of its own standards. Now that control of the State was no longer certain to be in Christian hands, a State connection seemed less important than it had once been. The Free Churches in various lands had justified their existence as spiritual forces. It had also become apparent in connection with the House of Lords case (1904) that glorying in spiritual freedom had perhaps led to the ignoring of certain facts with regard to the function of law. One must be related in some way to the State, and there are situations where the law must step in. The times were further laying a new emphasis upon community spirit and corporate life; and this brought with it new sympathy for the idea of national recognition of religion.

Some of the more conservative members of the Free Church had gone out after 1892 (Free Presbyterians) or in 1900 (present Free Church); and this reduced the dissimilarity between the Church of Scotland and the United Free Church. No one still survived in either body who had personal memories of the Disruption. The ministers of both Churches had taken the same Arts courses at the universities, and came to their Divinity training with the same outlook in philosophy and science. They read the same theological books, English and German. Differences of opinion were almost as great within one Church as between the two Churches. Both denominations had their Sunday Schools and Bible Classes, and used the same psalm tunes and the same hymn-book. Ordinary people connected themselves with the one or the other indifferently, and changed from one to the other at marriage or on removing to a new district or because attracted by the music or the preaching.

The 1914-18 War was another contributing influence. Chaplains at the front or in hospital were not recognised as belonging to Church of Scotland or United Free Church, but as Presbyterians; and the members of the two Churches on active service attended common services, while those at home had united prayer meetings and united gatherings at war memorials. Both Churches had the same problems to face in those critical days and the same consciousness that the religious opportunities of the time had not been very successfully seized. The post-war situation was even more challenging. Indifference to religion and carelessness about moral standards, a changed attitude towards all authority, the passion for amusement and the great extension of opportunities for sport and entertainment, anti-God Communism, decrease in church-going and Bible-reading and reverence for the Sunday, the non-Christian and anti-Christian novel and newspaper, were indications of a new world in face of whose problems the differences amongst the denominations appeared pathetically trifling. It was realised that a challenge, not to this or that Church, but to Christianity itself, had been thrown down. Many who were far from anxious for a Union between the Church of Scotland and the United Free Church felt that in the circumstances the existing divisions were unjustifiable, and that Union was a clear duty.

Some also had the altered financial situation in mind. Scotland could no longer afford the luxury of so many denominations. There was the pressing question of meeting the religious needs of a shifting population, the problem raised by the many rival churches in the villages and the few churches in the crowded industrial areas. The seriousness of the Home Mission challenge demanded Union. The position on the Foreign Mission Field was similar: the puzzling disunity which the pagan world had discovered amongst the professing followers of Jesus was plainly hampering the work.

Christians themselves were less absorbed than they had been in the details of belief and organisation and more interested in the great principles of the Christian Faith. As a result of theological and scientific and historical and psychological inquiry there was now a better understanding of what Christianity really is and means. The things which Christians treasured in common were coming to outweigh the things which kept them apart. The important matter clearly was that Christ should be shown forth that the world might believe.

The Churches Confer.—Already in 1907 the Church of Scotland, inspired by Dr Archibald Scott of St George's, Edinburgh, had appointed a Committee to inquire into the possibilities of Union. The Free Church and the United Free Church were invited to confer; and the latter agreed to enter into "unrestricted conference upon the whole ecclesiastical situation." The common difficulties of the two bodies were discussed and their common theological position was recognised; and by 1911 hopeful reports had been received by both Assemblies. It was obvious that the questions of Spiritual Independence and the National Recognition of Religion were crucial.

A 'Memorandum' by the Church of Scotland in 1912 stated the position of that Church in such terms as were acceptable to the United Free Church as a basis for more detailed discussion. Thereafter the Church of Scotland prepared Articles declaring its constitution. The Great War delayed matters; but ultimately the Articles were sent down under the Barrier Act to Church of Scotland Presbyteries in 1919, and approved by a very large majority. Parliament was then approached to make it legal for the Church to adopt these Articles, and an Act to this effect recognising the lawfulness of what the Church was claiming was passed in 1921.

The United Free Church heartily agreed that the Church of Scotland had thus obtained such State recognition of its spiritual independence that it was as free as any so-called free Church, without surrendering its position as a national Church. The Church of Scotland was satisfied that its action deprived it of nothing in the way of State connection that in modern conditions was ever likely to be helpful. An eminent English churchman, Lord Hugh Cecil, declared that the Act of 1921 " harmonises with a definiteness and completeness for which I think no parallel in Christian history is to be found, the National Recognition of Religion with the Spiritual Freedom of the Church."

There was still the question of endowments. Many parish ministers received at least part of their stipend from the 'teinds' or 'tithes.' The subject of teinds is one that is full of difficulties, both legal and historical. Perhaps it is enough for us to note that the teinds were " the proportion of the produce of the soil dedicated to religion from the time that land rights existed." Those who purchased land took over with it the responsibility of making certain payments to the church that was connected with the property. The United Free Church laid down as a condition of Union that " all the endowments of the Church of Scotland must be vested in it under a tenure which is consistent with the freedom set forth in the Articles and which recognises no right of the State to exercise any special control over the Church in virtue of its enjoyment of these endowments."

A Government Commission went into this question. Not only had the somewhat conflicting views of the two Churches to be reconciled, but the heritors or landowners who paid stipend from 'teind' had to be considered; and finally the recommendations had to run the gauntlet of discussion in Parliament. In the end an ideal arrangement from the Church point of view was not achieved, and the Church of Scotland lost about a sixth of the annual income that was involved; but most of the difficulties were overcome, and the United Free Church was satisfied with the Act of Parliament of 1925, according to which landowners were henceforth to make a fixed payment to the Church, this source of income being the absolute property of the Church "to be held and used by it in the religious interest of the nation and in the exercise of the powers and liberties set forth in the Articles of 1921." At the same time the church buildings and manses were declared to be the absolute property of the Church, and the heritors were relieved of the expense of upkeep.

The new constitution involving these Acts of 1921 and 1925 (the Declaratory Articles of the Church of Scotland, and the Property and Endowments Act) was accepted by the Church of Scotland in 1926; and a Committee of one hundred ministers and elders from each Church was appointed to discuss the Basis of Union. There were constant meetings of sub-committees, a great deal of discussion, many difficulties, and some misunderstandings. Words are always amongst the chief troubles on occasions of this sort, for different persons may use them in different senses. The word 'Establishment' was a case in point. A small section of the United Free Church, under the leadership of the Rev. James Barr, proved dissatisfied, and refused to compromise. Eventually they declined to accept the Union and are now known as the United Free Church.

In 1928 the proposed Basis and Plan of Union was sent down by the Assemblies under the Barrier Act, and it was found that the detailed scheme met with general approval amongst the members of the two Churches. With enthusiasm the Assemblies decided upon the Union of the Churches; and this was consummated on 2nd October 1929. The leaders to whom credit is mainly due for this wonderful achievement included, on the Church of Scotland side, Dr Archibald Scott and Lord Balfour of Burleigh, and later Dr Wallace Williamson of St Cuthbert's, Edinburgh, Dr John White of the Barony, Glasgow, and Lord Sands, a judge of the Court of Session; and on the United Free Church side, Dr Archibald Henderson of Crieff, Principal Martin of New College, Edinburgh, and Dr R. J. Drummond of Lothian Road Church, Edinburgh.

The Union Assembly.—At the Union Assembly in Edinburgh in October 1929 King George VI. (then Duke of York) acted as Lord High Commissioner representing his father. First of all the two Assemblies met separately and were constituted, and then the members left their respective halls in procession, and the two companies met and merged and marched together into St Giles's Cathedral. On the same day the united Assembly met in a huge motor garage which had been temporarily transformed into a hall accommodating 12,000 people. The gathering was one of the most brilliant, enthusiastic, solemn, and moving in the Church history of our land. The Church of Scotland and the United Free Church were declared to be one Church under the name of the Church of Scotland. Delegates from other Churches and public bodies offered their congratulations, and before the close of this historic Assembly many inspiring addresses were delivered, the last being that of the Archbishop of Canterbury.

It took more than twenty years to achieve this triumphant Union, and it has naturally taken some time for the two traditions to settle down together. The special characteristics of the uniting Churches have not been removed, but recognised as complementary to one another. The Union was not so much an end as a beginning; and all the strength and consecration of all the elements combined in the new body will be required in order to face the problems and tasks of the changed world in which we live. The reunited Church is very rich in experience, and it started its new life in a truly Christian desire for the well-being of Scotland and for the coming of the Kingdom. Our Church has undergone many transformations since the days of St Ninian, survived many disasters, has been guided to the accomplishment of much true service, and remains worthy of its motto: " Nec Tamen Consumebatur " (Exodus iii. 2).

Books to read :—

J. R. Fleming, 'The Story of Church Union in Scotland.' (1929.)
J. Buchan and G. A. Smith, 'The Kirk in Scotland, 1560-1929.' (1929.)

CHAPTER XXIII.

OUR OWN DAY.

The General Assembly.—"Take from us the freedom of Assemblies, and take from us the Evangel," said John Knox when on one occasion the existence of the Supreme Court of the Church was at stake. There were indeed considerable intervals in the seventeenth century during which no Assembly was held, for the institution was incompatible with absolutism; but since the close of that century the meetings have taken place annually. The General Assembly has amply justified itself by its works. It has had a great reputation as a representative body, and to-day includes in its membership in rotation about a quarter of the ministers of the Church, each accompanied by an elder, who may be nobleman, laird, burgess, or peasant, for the Kirk Sessions from which they come are composed of men from every class in society.

Early Assemblies were small, the first having had only about 40 members, while the famous Glasgow Assembly of 1638 was attended by some 140 ministers and 100 elders; and the critical Assembly of 1843 had 456 members. In recent times, partly on account of Church unions, numbers have greatly increased, and the membership each year must now be about 1600. The size of the gathering appears as an asset if one is thinking of the Assembly as an instrument of inspiration for the Church; but a very serious disadvantage if one remembers its function of discussion and legislation. There is no longer time for those speeches lasting several hours, which were once a proud feature of the meetings. Nor is there any possibility of more than a very few actually taking part in the proceedings. The social side of the Assembly fortnight has also greatly developed in recent times; and while this adds interest it interferes with business. The

Church has now a larger number of Committees which have to report to the Assembly. This annual meeting is also the occasion when inter-Church and international relations can most effectively be strengthened. It is extremely difficult to do justice in the two weeks to all interests; and the problem of how to make the best use of the venerable institution is serious.

Assemblies invariably meet in Edinburgh. In other days this was not the case, and important Assemblies have been held at Aberdeen, Perth, Dundee, and elsewhere. Early Secession Synods met at various centres. The Free Church had an Assembly in Inverness soon after the Disruption. The 1938 Assembly of the present Free Church took place in Glasgow. But the seat of government for the Church of Scotland is now definitely Edinburgh; and the solemn and dignified gatherings of the Assembly are amongst the Capital's proudest occasions.

The Assembly meetings have as their chairman the Moderator, whose title was adopted from France. He is technically elected by the Assembly; but actually selected some time previously by a Committee set up for the purpose. In theory he is only Moderator during the sittings of the Assembly, but in practice he is treated as the official representative of the Church for a complete year, and demits office when the next Assembly meets, having in the interval given his whole time to visiting parishes, addressing audiences, attending ceremonies, dedicating churches, presiding at meetings, voicing the opinion of the Church on important occasions, and in numerous ways acting as an encouragement and stimulus among the congregations.

At the Assembly meetings other officials are also in evidence —the Clerks, the Procurator, the Agent, the Leader of the Assembly, the Precentor, the Officer. The Acts, Proceedings, and Debates of the Assembly are recorded every year and fill a considerable volume.

Most of the speaking is actually done by ministers; but one of the most important features of the Assembly is that there are as many laymen as ministers in its membership, and the layman has full liberty of speech on any subject, and his vote has the same weight as that of a minister. Only elders can be lay members of Assembly.

The State is represented at the meetings by the King's Lord High Commissioner specially appointed for the occasion. Different views of his function have naturally prevailed in different periods. Thus it was the King who summoned the Glasgow Assembly of 1638, and his Commissioner endeavoured to guide the business and eventually declared the Court dissolved; but the members continued in session and transacted business after the Commissioner's departure, on the ground that Assemblies were for the Church to arrange or at least that the King's part was finished when he had summoned the Assembly and seen it duly constituted, although it has to be noted that the Church acquiesced in the formal authorisation of the transactions of 1638 by the 1639 Assembly at which the Commissioner was present. There was long a difference of opinion as to whether the Church or the State had the duty and right of calling Assemblies. The tradition in favour of the State began with the Emperor Constantine in 325 A.D. As far as Scotland is concerned, the matter was finally settled in 1928 in favour of the Church.

The King's Commissioner interests himself in the business, but does not interfere. He is not by virtue of his office a member of the Assembly, and has no vote. His presence at the meetings of Assembly is on account of the continued recognition of the Church of Scotland as the National Church, and the admitted obligation of the sovereign to "maintain and preserve the settlement of the true Protestant religion with the government, worship, discipline, and privileges of the Church of Scotland." A representative of the King would be welcome at any public function; but it is not without importance that the State is still thus officially willing to recognise religion by being represented at the Church of Scotland General Assembly.

The Assembly remains the chief Court of the Church. Synods meet half-yearly, and Presbyteries as a rule have an ordinary meeting each month, while Kirk Sessions, the fourth of the Church Courts which are of the essence of Presbyterian government, meet monthly or as often as congregational business demands.

The Work of the Church.—Much of the work of the Church, however, at the present day devolves upon Committees selected by Assembly to supervise the many 'Schemes.'

The early nineteenth century was familiar with the 'Five Schemes'; but the number presently increased and the operations expanded. The twentieth century has witnessed the rapid intensification of this process and has seen the appointment of permanent Secretaries and Deputies; and the Offices of the Church of Scotland at 121 George Street, Edinburgh, have become the headquarters of a great business firm as well as of a powerful spiritual agency. Both the organization and the finance of the Church have grown in complication. Change in financial methods may be indicated by mentioning the Freewill Offering Scheme of recent years. The expenditure of all great organizations—the government of the country, education, local government, national defence—has in our time increased beyond all comparison with what was ample provision in earlier periods. Similar conditions govern the management of the Church. Its widespread activities may best be judged from the detailed information to be found in the Church of Scotland Year-Book, in the annual volume of the Reports to the General Assembly, and in the pages of 'Life and Work,' the monthly magazine of the Church.

The expense of ordinary congregational existence has increased, salaries, music, furnishings, decoration, organizations, maintenance of halls, and everything about churches being on a higher standard than formerly. Responsibility for a congregation's finances is at present in the hands of a Congregational Board, or Deacons' Court, or Committee of Management, or Kirk Session, the variety being due to pre-union conditions: uniformity of practice will no doubt come. With regard to the raising of money both for congregational and for general Church purposes, one cannot overlook the useful part played by the Woman's Guilds.

In connection with work in the foreign field, costs have inevitably increased; but the condition of the modern world makes it more than ever a pressing Christian obligation to show forth Christ, and the Church is gallantly facing the heavy financial strain both on its general Foreign Mission funds and on those of the Women's Association. Never were missionary ideals higher. Work among the Jews, in strengthening ties with continental Churches, and in meeting the spiritual needs of our fellow-countrymen in other lands, is in present circumstances more worth while than ever before, and calls for the sympathy of every congregation and member.

Post-war Home Mission problems are many. The most outstanding is perhaps the necessity of church extension in new housing schemes and in crowded industrial areas. There is, on the other hand, a continued call for union of congregations in districts where the population does not justify the existence of several churches of the same denomination. Work has to be done by way of providing halls, especially in country places where the community spirit and the demand for social facilities have vastly increased; arranging religious services at outlying stations; missions amongst fishermen and fisher girls, summer campers and visitors to seaside resorts, berry-pickers, city lodging-house dwellers, and others. The sparsely populated Highlands and Islands present special problems.

The Church is finding it necessary to attempt to help classes of people whose distress results largely from the defective Christianity of the community as a whole. It does not lose sight of its main object, which is to save souls and so to render people fit to face any conditions; but it also recognises its duty to strengthen and uplift, to foster well-being and make life richer. In 1910 the Church of Scotland formed a Social Work Committee, and now provides Homes for children, working lads or girls, unfortunates of various types, and the aged. More recently the Church and Nation Committee has undertaken responsibility "to watch over developments of the Nation's life in which moral and spiritual considerations specially arise and to consider what action the Church from time to time may be advised to take to further the highest interests of the people." It deals with such matters as betting and gambling, the Church's attitude to war, the obstacles to Sunday observance. The present is full of challenges for the Church. Problems of detail, such as the possibility of new methods suggested by the development of cinema and wireless, have to be examined, and the Church has to reckon with world movements, the new fact of anti-Christian states and communities, the present-day journalistic and fictional ethics, modern scientific and economic attitudes, the new psychology, and much else that is, or thinks itself, new. The modern situation is one which challenges the Church to the dedication of all its resources.

The Responsibility of a National Church.—Though all baptized persons are members of the Church, only those who are communicants have their names upon the church roll, and have full rights, for example, in the election of ministers. The healthiest congregations are those where the largest proportion of those connected with the Church are not merely earnestly receptive but are actively interested in its work. The Church now makes heavy financial demands upon its members. One result is apt to be that it may lose hold of that large section of the population which is friendly but will never be enthusiastic. People should not be driven by the Church into the arms of the enemy. The National Church has a duty not only to those who give and serve gladly, but to all who are willing to listen to its message even though their response is of the feeblest. It dare not permit whole classes to slip from its influence; and it must continue to demand the attention and to force itself upon the notice of those who least eagerly seek after its ministrations or join in its activities. There should always be an open door and a free Gospel. The Church of Scotland works upon a territorial basis; but the incessant demands for attention on the part of the faithful and active make it far from easy for ministers to give so much time as they might to those who are in deepest need of their help; and the parochial system offers peculiar difficulties in the cities. Responsibility involves readiness to adapt oneself to new conditions. The Church showed this spirit in appointing the commission which in 1946 issued the report, 'God's Will for Church and Nation,' and in the encouragement it has given to the Iona Community. To-day there is pressing need for the layman to realise his obligation to be an evangelist.

The Ministry.—Provision for the ministry is under the care of the Maintenance of the Ministry Committee, while training is supervised by the Committee on Education for the Ministry.

The Presbyterian Churches in Scotland have consistently demanded a high standard of educational equipment in those preparing for the ministry. After leaving school all attended an Arts Course at a university for three or four years, and then began the course in Divinity. Students of the Presbyterian bodies outwith the Church of Scotland mostly attended

Theological Colleges provided by their denomination. The Church of Scotland students continued to make use of the university Divinity Faculties, where the professors were all ministers of their Church, but neither appointed nor paid by the Church. In the universities during the later eighteenth century and much of the nineteenth the Divinity course occupied three or four years if students made this their whole-time employment during the winter months. It was, however, permissible to attend for one complete session and then to give 'partial' attendance for five or six sessions, and the majority of the prospective ministers seem to have taken advantage of this, since it enabled them to make a living as teachers, working at their studies in spare hours and then going to the university for a few weeks in the year and delivering one of the fairly serious exercises which formed part of the requirements. In those days there were more than sufficient candidates for the ministry in all the churches, and this kept the standard of attainment high. The ministry was in great esteem as a profession; those best equipped mentally and spiritually turned eagerly to it; and schoolmasters did much to encourage the brightest pupils to aim at serving the Church.

The degree of Bachelor of Divinity (B.D.) was instituted by the universities, and the number of professorships increased in accordance with the modern demand for specialisation. The most recent change has been the creation at all the centres of professorships in Practical Training. The Union of the Churches in 1929 brought about a combination of the universities and the Church Colleges in the education of Divinity students. The course now includes at least three years in Arts and three in Divinity. The Church of Scotland needs to-day more candidates for the ministry than are offering. The ministry is a calling that holds out small worldly inducements, but to those with the highest motives it presents a great opportunity for true and happy service.

Youth.—Nothing is more hopeful for the future of the Church than the success that attends its activities amongst the young. John Calvin and John Knox recognised the supreme importance of such work. To-day anti-Christian Communistic zeal energetically follows the same path. Everyone realises that for the triumph of any cause the support of youth must be enlisted. The Church of Scotland has developed and improved its Sunday School system on sound modern lines, supplying the necessary literature and training of teachers, and providing for advanced work in Bible Classes and allied youth organisations. Every opportunity is certainly available for young people to develop themselves, express themselves, enjoy themselves. The future will depend upon the use which they make of what the past has provided for them in producing so many initial advantages, and upon the response which they may prove strong enough and brave enough and consecrated enough to make to the challenge that their new world presents.

Books to read :—

G. D. Henderson, 'The Claims of the Church of Scotland.' (1951.)
G. D. Henderson, 'Why we are Presbyterians.' (1953.)
A. H. Dunnett, 'The Church in Changing Scotland.'

CHAPTER XXIV.

THE PRESBYTERIAN FAMILY.

Our Calvinistic Heritage.—The Church of Scotland belongs to the group of Churches which accepted the Reformation in the sixteenth century. These had a common reverence for the Bible and a common ambition to be true to its guidance in doctrine, worship, Church government, and discipline. For a time these Churches held fairly well together. The universities all used the Latin language. Students therefore went from one country to another, studying as conveniently in a foreign land as at home; and there was thus amongst the leaders of the various Churches a similarity of experience and outlook that no longer persists.

Calvin and Beza were consulted by letter on Scottish Church affairs. The Scots General Assembly was asked for and gave its approval to the Second Helvetic Confession adopted at Zurich in 1566. A number of Scots ministered in French churches and others taught in French Colleges. Samuel Rutherfurd was more than once invited to accept a professorship in a Dutch university. The delegates to the Westminster Assembly kept in touch with continental Churches: in 1644 we find them sending an official friendly letter to the Reformed Churches in Holland, France, and Switzerland. Continental students sometimes studied in Scotland and many Scottish names appear in the lists of Leyden, Marburg, and other foreign universities. The different Churches were in contact with one another.

The Reformation, however, being a revolt from authority, favoured independence both in peoples and amongst persons, and so encouraged nationalism and individualism. Unfortunately although this makes for progress, it tends to produce separation and difference ; and the Protestant Churches have latterly become very provincial and isolated. There has been a want of unity, friendship, and co-operation. Each has been left to face its problems without much sympathy and support from others. This has been a source of weakness, particularly in countries where Protestantism has a struggling existence in a Romish or anti-Christian environment.

The Church of Scotland is one of the strongest Presbyterian Churches in the world. If it took a greater interest in its sister Churches in other lands it could inspire and develop some of the weaker Churches, with benefit to the Presbyterian and Reformed cause in general and with real effect upon the peace of Europe and the world, and there would be a favourable reaction upon its own life. We ought to know something of the other Protestant Churches. Especially should we have some acquaintance with those of the Presbyterian family. They are nearer to us than Lutherans, Baptists, or Anglicans, and share with us the Calvinistic tradition.

John Calvin was a Frenchman, but settled in Geneva. In his 'Institutes' he set forth a complete theological system, not departing from the teaching of the authorised creeds of the whole Christian Church, but emphasising specially the sovereignty of God, free grace, the corruption of human nature, predestination, and election. He laid the foundations of Presbyterian Church government, abandoning the old clerical rule and giving the layman a new share in Church life. A simple form of service was introduced with psalm-singing, scripture-reading, informal prayers, and a great deal of preaching. There was strict discipline, moral and social, with a carefully guarded Sunday, the aim being to make and keep Christian the whole life of the community, including trade, politics, private life, recreation, international relations.

John Knox was a disciple of Calvin and introduced his system into Scotland in 1560. It appealed to other countries also, and especially to nations or persons that were making a struggle for independence. Scotland had at first to contend against French penetration and domination ; and later against English interference and misgovernment. Holland had to free itself from Spain. Hungary had the Turks to face and the Hapsburgs to suffer. The strength of Cromwell's Ironsides was derived from Calvinism. The early settlers in the New England States succeeded in their valiant enterprise through the qualities which sprang from their Calvinistic faith. Calvinism has been called "the seed-bed of Liberty."

Calvinism has been one of the main influences in advancing Democracy in many lands. It taught the equality of all before God, all having sinned and being equally dependent upon the Grace of God. It gave an impetus to Education, for it demanded of people an intelligent interest in their religion and regarded them as entitled to instruction and guidance. It encouraged the idea that life is a trust from God, and that men are called to serve God in their ordinary occupations. It laid stress upon duty and industry; and its discipline produced backbone and grit so that Calvinistic peoples prospered both spiritually and materially.

Presbyterianism on the Continent.—From Geneva strong influence was exerted upon France. The first Protestant service was held in Paris in 1555. A Confession of Faith and a Scheme of Discipline were accepted in 1559 when the first National Synod met. The complete Presbyterian system as we now know it in Scotland with Assembly, Synod, Presbytery, and Kirk Session came to us from France. Great leaders were Theodore Beza, the successor of Calvin (1519-1605); Admiral Coligny (1519-1572), who was amongst the many thousands of victims in the massacre of Protestants on St Bartholomew's Day, 1572; and Henry IV. (1589-1610), who, though brought up a Protestant, became a Romanist to secure himself on the throne of France, but gave religious liberty to the Huguenots (as the French Protestants were called) by the Edict of Nantes, 1598. The French Reformed Church remained a minority; but it was very enterprising, establishing Colleges and developing a remarkably prosperous community. There had been intermittent civil war between Romanists and Protestants till the Edict, and it was not very long after that event till persecution arose, growing in terrible severity until in 1685, when Louis XIV. revoked the Edict, the remaining Huguenots were driven from the country or exterminated. French Protestantism has never fully recovered.

After a long interval during which it could only exist in the strictest secrecy, a certain revival began in the eighteenth century under Antoine Court; and after the French Revolution, which began in 1789, Napoleon granted liberty of conscience to Protestants once more. Presbyterians in France, like those in other lands, have shown a tendency to divide; and, though an interesting Union was recently consummated, they are not yet all within a single Church. French Presbyterians, however, form a healthy, though not very large, Evangelical body, which needs our sympathy in its efforts to uphold Protestantism in a country that is formally Romanist but largely anti-Christian.

Equally interesting is the Church in Holland, which was closely associated with the successful struggle of the Dutch to free their country from Spain in the sixteenth century. Their leader was William the Silent (1533-1584). After liberty had been obtained and the Protestant faith established, the Dutch Church had to face the troublesome problem of the relations of Church and State, and later strong differences of opinion developed with regard to Doctrine, the strict Calvinists succeeding in crushing the liberal Arminians at the Synod which met at Dort in 1618.

In Holland during the seventeenth century there was an enormous output of theological literature, and Scottish ministers were as familiar with Dutch learning as they were with English. Many Scots received part of their education in Holland, and many more lived there in exile during the religious troubles of that period. In the nineteenth century the Dutch Church suffered more than one Secession, and to-day two Presbyterian bodies are outstanding. The Reformed Church of the Netherlands (Hervormde Kerk) is the National Church, and much the larger denomination. The smaller body, the Reformed Churches of the Netherlands (Gereformeerde Kerken) is more like the Free Church of Scotland in its strict Calvinism and Puritanism, and has exercised powerful influence for its size, having instituted the Free University of Amsterdam and having in the person of Abraham Kuyper (died 1920) given Holland a minister of religion as Prime Minister.

Germany was chiefly reformed by Luther; but the influence of Calvin was also felt. Heidelberg, for example, was a strong Presbyterian centre. The 'Heidelberg Catechism,' adopted in 1563, is generally regarded as in many respects the most satisfying of all the Reformed Confessional documents. It was long taught to students in the Scottish universities. In present-day Germany there are many Calvinists, including leaders of the Confessional Churches who found themselves unable to accept the principles of Hitler.

In Bohemia and Moravia there was an early movement for reform under John Hus, who was burnt at the stake by order of the Church Council of Constance in 1415. His memory has never died, and Protestantism has always maintained its appeal. It was almost crushed out of being as a result of the battle of the White Mountain in 1620, and had a struggling existence under Austrian rule until after the Great War (1914-1918), when a considerable section of the people severed their connection with the Church of Rome. There are now several healthy Protestant Churches; but recent political events are putting a severe strain upon them, and they require all the support we can give them. The Evangelical Church of Czech Brethren, with which the first President of Czecho-Slovakia, Dr Thomas Masaryk, identified himself, has marked Presbyterian features, and for long had close and friendly relations with our Scottish Church.

Presbyterianism is one of the most powerful forces in modern Hungary. The population is predominantly Romanist, but the influence of the Presbyterian section is strong out of all proportion to its size. Great leaders of the nation have been associated with this body. Many Magyar-speaking Presbyterians now live in territory outside the boundaries of political Hungary, particularly in the Transylvanian part of Roumania; but they adhere firmly to their old traditions. In Hungary the 'Heidelberg Catechism' (1563) and the 'Second Helvetic Confession' (1566) were adopted in 1567. The chief centre of Calvinistic activity was Debrecen, and the strength of Presbyterianism lay in the north-eastern provinces and on the Great Plain. The Hungarian Church has been keenly Evangelical and orthodox. It has done much for peasant education, for thrift, for industry, and for moral strength. Many of its ministers have received part of their education in Scotland or in Holland. An unusual feature is that though ardently Presbyterian this Church has bishops.

Switzerland is a country very much divided. Some cantons speak German, some French, one Italian. Similarly some cantons are mainly Protestant, others mainly Romanist. The Protestants have been largely of the Calvinistic tradition, but differences crept in amongst them in the nineteenth century, and it is only recently that they have drawn more closely together again and have entered into a common Federation.

The ancient and famous Waldensian Church in Italy is small but energetic. Protestantism has more opportunity of developing in present-day Italy than it had in earlier centuries. There are also Presbyterians in Belgium, Rumania, Greece, Spain, Portugal, and also in other lands.

Presbyterianism in the Empire and Beyond.—Calvinism in the Reformation period was favourably received in England. It was the inspiration of Puritanism, and has left its mark upon the Thirty-nine Articles of the Church of England. The growth of Independency lessened the influence of Presbyterianism, and for a time it almost died out. Only in the nineteenth century did it revive. The United Presbyterian Church of Scotland formed many congregations south of the border, and other Scottish Churches were set up. In 1876 the various Presbyterian bodies united to form the Presbyterian Church of England, combining the English Puritan and the Scottish traditions. There are still some congregations directly connected with the Church of Scotland, including St Columba's, London. It should be remembered to what an extent we owe to English Presbyterians the Westminster Confession, the Shorter Catechism, and the metrical psalms.

There is a strong Presbyterian Church in Northern Ireland, ardently Protestant and devoted to the Reformed standards. It owes something to the immigrants from Scotland in the seventeenth century.

The Welsh Presbyterian Church is partly the outcome of the work of George Whitefield, the famous Methodist preacher (died 1770), and was for long called the Calvinistic Methodist Connection. It is intensely Welsh in character; but has latterly drawn closer to other members of the Presbyterian family.

In the British Dominions and Colonies Presbyterianism

has been deeply planted and extensively spread by Scottish settlers. There are flourishing Presbyterian Churches in Australia, New Zealand, South Africa, and elsewhere. Canada has now the Presbyterian Church in Canada, and also the United Church of Canada which includes Presbyterians along with Congregationalists and Methodists. Effective Presbyterian congregations are to be found in Argentine, British Guiana, the West Indies, Malaya, and in other places where enterprising Scots have made their homes. Perhaps the Church could do more to encourage Church life amongst our Scottish kinsfolk at the ends of the earth. They are of our household, they have peculiar temptations to face, they are often few and so unable to provide for Church ordinances, or they may be careless and require a lead in the matter. By their way of life, too, the wide world judges not only us at home, but also Christ Himself. It is important for us to think of these things.

Nowhere has Presbyterianism thriven better than in the United States. Many of the early settlers were fervent Puritans who left England in the early seventeenth century to seek religious liberty across the Atlantic. The first Presbytery was that of Philadelphia, formed in 1706. In the huge area now covered by the States there are several great Presbyterian Churches, including not only those of British, but others of Dutch and German origin. Amongst them they have between two and three million members.

Other groups of Presbyterians in various parts of the world—China, Japan, India, Africa—are the results of modern Foreign Mission endeavour.

We must remember further that in Scotland there are Presbyterians outside the Church of Scotland—the Reformed Presbyterian, Original Secession, Free, Free Presbyterian, and United Free Churches. These Churches have a small membership; but they are all earnest in their Presbyterianism.

Through its Continental and Colonial Committee the Church of Scotland endeavours to keep up relations with Presbyterians in other lands. It gives financial help to those in difficulties; the ministers of its own congregations on the Continent co-operate with the native Presbyterian Churches;

it invites foreign students to its Divinity Halls; it sends delegates to meetings abroad to help in developing the family feeling; and it asks representatives of other Churches to address our General Assembly. This is work of a very valuable type and ought to be attempted on a much larger scale for our own good and that of World Presbyterianism. Unity is strength.

Œcumenical Movements.—In 1875 a movement which has great possibilities was begun by the formation of the Presbyterian Alliance, whose purpose is to enable the Reformed Churches to develop a common feeling among themselves and to speak and act in harmony, to enable the strong to help the weak, and to put the thought and experience of each Church at the service of all. Conferences are held at regular intervals in America, on the Continent, or in Britain. The headquarters of the Alliance are in Geneva.

Recent world developments have produced in various countries powerful anti-Christian forces, which threaten to corrupt or to destroy the Church of Christ. The danger is serious, and it is becoming more and more necessary for Christians of all denominations to realise their common interests and to offer a common front to the enemies of Christian principle. The special tenets of the particular religious body in which we have been brought up are naturally important for us, and we shall not underestimate their value nor cease to be proud of the history which has put us in the position of offering our special contribution to the Fulness of Christ. On the other hand, it is even more important that we should remember our claim to be part of the one Body of Christ, and our belief in "one Lord, one Faith, one Baptism, one God and Father of all."

In view of the modern world situation Protestant Churches have been drawing together. The World Missionary Conference at Edinburgh in 1910 was one of the earliest expressions of this helpful tendency. After a World Conference at Copenhagen in 1922 the Central Office for Inter-Church Aid was constituted at Geneva to give practical expression to the sense of Protestant solidarity. Conferences on 'Faith and Order' at Lausanne (1927) and Edinburgh (1937) and on 'Life and Work' at Stockholm (1925) and Oxford (1937) fostered a better understanding amongst the many Churches of many countries which participated, and led to the epoch-making foundation of the World Council of Churches at Amsterdam in 1948. In all this work the Church of Scotland plays an honourable part.

Books to read:—

J. N. Ogilvie, 'The Presbyterian Churches of Christendom.' (1925 edition.)

G. D. Henderson, 'Presbyterianism.' (1954.)

INDEX

Abbeys, 26 ff., 36.
Aberdeen Doctors, 69, 73, 91.
Aberdeen, King's College Church, 29 f.
Adamnan, St, 16 ff.
Andrew, St, 6, 23.
Architecture, 3, 28 f., 86, 145 f., 159, 167.
Assembly, General, 5, 59, 60, 61, 65, 69, 74, 89, 94, 95, 96, 97 f., 103, 104 f., 110, 115 f., 178 ff.
Associate Presbytery (Synod), 106 ff., 111 f.
Auchterarder Case, 136 ff.

Baillie, Robert, 72.
Baird Trust, 156.
Balfour, Lord, of Burleigh, 158, 176.
Baptism, 18, 31, 33, 52, 65, 72, 87, 97, 193.
Barrier Act, 98.
Beaton, Cardinal, 25, 44.
Begg, James, 149.
Bible, 17, 24, 39 ff., 42 f., 48 f., 51, 53, 61, 70, 72, 74, 75, 84, 86, 88, 89, 91, 97, 105, 115, 131, 147 f., 149, 157, 163, 164, 165, 169, 186.
Bible Class, 3, 5, 147, 169, 173, 185.
Binning, Hew, 90.
Bishop, 11, 20 f., 25, 35, 57 f., 60, 64, 65, 69, 75, 80, 94
Blackadder, John, 78 f.
Blair, Hugh, 113.
Blathmac, Abbot, 22.
Book of Common Order, 51, 53 f., 61, 72.
Boston, Thomas, 99, 102, 117, 119.
Brown, John, of Broughton, 129, 130, 132.
Brown, John, of Priesthill, 81 f.
Bruce, King Robert, 35 f.
Bruce, Master Robert, 90.
Burghers and Anti-Burghers, 108, 116, 122, 129.

Cairns, John, 130 f., 132.
Calvin, John, 3, 41, 47, 48 f., 51, 53, 58, 70, 88, 97, 101 f., 103, 112, 132, 140, 148, 157, 165, 166, 169, 171, 184, 186, 187, 188 ff.
Cameron, Richard, 80.
Cameronians, 81, 94, 97, 101.
Campbell, John Macleod, 52, 119.
Candida Casa, 12 f., 16, 22.
Candlish, R. S., 139, 141, 144, 166.
Canon Law, 25, 31, 38.
Cargill, Donald, 81.
Carlyle, Alexander, 114, 122.
Carstares, William, 93, 98, 106.
Catechism, Shorter, 54, 71 f., 75, 88, 98, 157, 164, 169, 191.
Cathedrals, 25, 28 f., 36.
Celtic Church, 9, 12, 19 ff., 26.

Chalmers, Thomas, 6, 121, 123, 127, 134, 138, 141, 142, 143 ff., 146, 147, 153, 161.
Chapel Act, 135 f., 141, 155.
Charles, King, I., 66, 69, 70 f., 73, 74.
Charles, King, II., 74, 76, 77, 81.
Charteris, A. H., 168.
Christmas, 26, 65, 167.
Church and State, 18, 21, 33, 51, 60, 63, 64, 67, 69, 83, 94, 99, 103, 125, 135 ff., 140, 142, 172.
Church Extension, 119, 144, 147, 174, 182.
Church Government, 3, 49, 61, 66, 71, 97 f., 99 f., 140, 146, 180, 186 f.
Church of Scotland, *passim*.
Church Union, 129, 132 f., 149 f., 158, 170 ff., 178, 184.
Civil Magistrate, 59 f., 72, 111.
Claim of Right (1689), 94.
Claim of Right (1842), 139 ff.
Collegiate Churches, 36 f.
Columba, St, 3, 5, 12, 14 ff., 22.
Commissioner, Lord High, 180.
Communion, 4, 24, 26, 32, 47, 52 f., 65, 72, 87 ff., 96, 99, 105, 112, 117, 167, 183.
Conventicles, 78 ff.
Cooper, James, 159.
Covenant, Covenanters, &c., 5, 64, 65, 67 ff., 70 f., 73 ff., 77 ff., 82 ff., 91, 99, 106, 108, 111, 141, 147, 166.
Creed, 3, 8, 26, 31, 45, 52 f., 75, 87, 97, 146.
Culdees, 25.
Cunningham, William, 139, 141, 145.
"Curates," The, 77 ff., 83, 95, 154.

David, King, I., 25, 27, 29.
Deacons, 4, 53, 59, 61, 181.
Dickson, David, 74, 90 f.
Directory for Public Worship, 53, 71 f., 87, 97, 121, 159.
Discipline, 3, 59, 61, 88, 110, 164 f., 188.
Discipline, First Book of, 52 f., 60.
Discipline, Second Book of, 52, 59 f.
Disestablishment, 129, 149 f., 158, 172, 176.
Disruption, 5, 103, 134 ff., 143 ff., 150 f., 153, 155, 158, 161, 163, 165, 173, 179.
Doctrine, 3, 32, 48, 51 f., 72, 75, 91, 99, 101 f., 106 f., 108, 115, 132, 148 f., 163, 168 f., 173, 186 f., 189.
Drummond, Henry, 147.
Duff, Alexander, 123.
Dunlop, A. M., 140, 145.
Durham, James, 90 f., 117, 131.

Easter, 20, 26, 65, 167.
Education, 34, 36, 39, 52, 58, 60, 61, 89, 146, 155, 156, 157, 163 f., 188.
Elders, 4, 52 f., 59 ff., 69, 71, 86 f., 89, 97, 105, 107, 115, 131, 142, 143, 147, 161, 164, 165, 168, 176, 178 f.
Elphinstone, Bishop, 25, 37.
Episcopacy, 47, 51, 57, 59 f., 64 f., 68 f., 70 f., 73, 74 ff., 77 ff., 82 f., 85, 91, 93 ff., 100, 101, 103, 154, 164, 166.
Erastianism, 63, 103, 137.
Erskine, Ebenezer, 6, 103, 105 f.
Erskine, John, of Dun, 48.
Erskine, Dr John, 112, 113, 122.
Erskine, Ralph, 103, 107, 119.
Evangelicals, 101, 103, 106, 111 f., 115 f., 117 ff., 129, 134 ff., 140, 144 f., 150, 153, 166.
"Exercise," The, 61.

Fisher, James, 105, 132.
" Five Articles of Perth," 65.
Forbes, John, of Corse, 73, 91.
" Forty Thieves," The, 139.
Free Church (1843), 108, 131 f., 140, 142, 143 ff., 153, 154, 156, 166, 169, 172, 179.
Free Church (1900), 151, 173 f., 179, 192.
Free Church Case, 150 f., 172.
Free Presbyterian Church, 149, 173, 192.
French Revolution, 118 f.

Gib, Adam, 108.
Gillespie, George, 72 f., 91.
Gillespie, Thomas, 110 f.
Glasgow Assembly (1638), 178, 180.
Graham of Claverhouse, 80, 96 f.
Guthrie, James, 74 f., 90.
Guthrie, Thomas, 145 f.

Haldane, R. and J., 120.
Hamilton, Archbishop, 44 f.
Hamilton, Patrick, 42.
Henderson, Alexander, 6, 52, 65, 68 ff., 72, 106.
Highlands, 97, 98, 149, 165, 182.
Home, John, 110, 114.
Hymns, 132, 165, 173.

Indulgences, 79, 83, 97.
Industrial Revolution, 118.
Instrumental Music, 159, 165 f.
Inverkeithing Case, 110.
Iona, 16, 17 ff., 22 f., 29, 183.

Jacobites, 96, 103, 154.
James, King, I., 36.
James, King, IV., 36.
James, King, V., 46, 55.
James, King, VI., 56, 60, 63 f., 69.
James, King, VII. (II.), 75, 81, 82 f., 93 f., 96, 128.
Johnston, Arch., of Wariston, 68 f., 72, 74 f.
" Judicial Testimony," The, 106.

Kennedy, Bishop, 37.
Kennedy, Dr John, 149.
Kentigern, St, 15.
Ker, Dr John, 131.
Kirk Session, 4, 59 ff., 73, 75, 86 ff., 97, 135, 163 f., 168, 178, 180.
Knox, John, 5, 6, 41, 42, 43, 44, 46 ff., 56 f., 60, 64, 67, 78, 84, 90, 97, 121, 157, 166, 178, 184, 187.

Lamberton, Bishop, 25, 35.
Laud, Archbishop, 66 f., 69, 75, 171.
" Lecture," The, 86, 97, 99, 165.
Lee, Robert, 158 f., 165 f.
Leighton, Robert, 75, 91.
Liturgy, 3, 31, 53, 67, 72, 75, 97, 159, 166.
Lord's Prayer, 26, 45, 53, 75, 87, 97.
Lyndsay, Sir David, 43.

Macdonald, Dr John, 149.
M'Lachlan, Margaret, 81.
Macleod, Norman, 6, 160.
Maelruhba, St, 15.
Margaret, Queen, 23 ff.
Marnoch Case, 137 f.
" Marrow Men," The, 102 f.
Martin, St, of Tours, 9 f., 11 f., 14.
Mary, Queen of Scots, 49, 55 f.
Melville, Andrew, 6, 52, 58 f., 60, 63 ff., 103, 140.
Metrical Psalms, 48, 53, 71 f., 75, 86, 88, 89, 97, 98, 165, 173, 191.

Middle Ages, 25, 27 f., 31 f., 33 f., 38, 63, 140.
Miller, Hugh, 145, 155.
Minister, 3, 5, 20, 25 f., 59, 60 f., 74, 85 f., 89, 90, 99, 108, 114, 115, 131.
Missions, Colonial, 147. 157. 181, 192.
Missions, Continental, 147, 181, 192.
Missions, Foreign, 4, 8, 12 f., 121 ff., 131, 146 f., 156 f., 174, 181, 193.
Missions, Home, 174, 182.
Missions, Jewish, 121, 146 f., 157, 181.
Moderates, 101, 106, 109, 112 ff., 119, 122 f., 134 f., 140, 151, 166.
Moderator of General Assembly, 4, 179.
Moluag, St, 15.
Monasticism, Monks, &c., 3, 9, 17 f., 20, 26 f., 31, 34, 38, 40.
Moncrieff, Alexander, 105.
Moncrieff, Sir Henry, 119 f.
Montrose, Marquis of, 73.
Moray, Regent, 48, 56.
Morison, James, 132.

National Recognition of Religion, 94 f., 125, 154, 174, 180.
Ninian, St, 5, 10 ff., 177.

Œcumenical Movements, 193 f.
Organisations, Congregational, 4, 167 f.
Oxford Movement, 138 f.

Parish, 25, 40, 50, 52, 59, 61, 78, 85 ff., 88 f., 95 f., 104, 107 f., 109, 127, 135 f., 141, 143, 153, 154, 156, 157, 160, 161, 163, 164, 175.
Patronage, 85, 101, 103 f., 106 f., 109, 114, 116, 134, 139 f., 149, 151, 156, 172.
Peden, Alexander, 81.
Poor, Care of, 24, 34, 60, 86, 89, 143, 155, 163.
Prayer Book (Laud's), 67.
Praying Societies, 107, 119.
Preaching, 18, 25, 47, 49, 50, 53, 75, 86, 88, 89 ff., 99, 105, 160, 166.
Presbyterianism, *passim*.
Presbyterianism Abroad, 91 f., 188 ff.
Presbytery, 4, 60 f., 75, 83, 89, 97 f., 99, 104, 110, 135, 136, 157, 180.
Protesters, 73 f., 101.
Puritanism, 66, 70, 71 f., 74, 85, 91, 97, 102, 115, 166, 189, 191.

Quoad Sacra Parishes, 135, 155, 156, 172.

Rainy, Principal, 150 ff.
Reformation, 3, 38 ff., 46 ff., 49 ff., 56, 58, 61 f., 63, 65 f., 67, 88, 92, 94, 128, 147, 154, 157, 186 f.
Relief Church, 109 ff., 116, 120, 129, 130, 165.
Renwick, James, 82, 140.
Resolutioners, 73, 74 f., 101.
Revolution Settlement, 93 ff., 103, 154.
"Riding Committees," 104, 109 f.
Robertson, Dr James, 155 f.
Robertson, Principal William, 6, 110, 112 f., 116.
Romanism, &c., 31 f., 33, 35, 40, 47, 48, 51, 55 f., 64, 65 ff., 68, 75, 76, 83, 86, 92, 93, 94, 101, 116, 128 f., 164, 187, 188, 190, 191.

Rutherfurd, Samuel, 72 f., 74, 90, 121, 140, 186.

Sacraments, 26, 32, 45, 53, 72, 89, 159.
Sands, Lord, 158, 176.
Scots Confession (1560), 51 f., 72.
Schemes of the Church, 146 f., 157, 180 ff.
Secessions, 5, 101 ff., 117 f., 125, 130, 136, 163.
Sharp, Archbishop, 75, 80.
Simson, Professor John, 101 f., 106.
Smith, Professor Robertson, 148, 151.
Spiritual Freedom, 67, 69, 83, 84, 106 f., 110, 140, 143 ff., 174.
Spottiswoode, Archbishop, 37, 91.
Sunday Observance, 53, 70, 72, 87, 147, 149, 161, 169, 173, 182.
Sunday Schools, 88, 120, 143, 147, 161, 168, 173, 185.
Superintendents, 52, 64, 66.
Superstitions, 26, 32, 38, 66, 89.
Synod, 60 f., 75, 83, 97, 180.

Teinds, 127, 175.
Toleration, 95 f., 103, 106, 115 f., 129, 140, 146, 172.
Training for the Ministry, 13, 52, 58, 90, 107, 111, 146, 157 f., 173, 183.
Tulloch, Principal John, 159.

United Free Church (1900), 133, 150 f., 172, 173 ff., 174 ff.
United Free Church (1929), 176, 192.
United Presbyterian Church, 108, 111, 125, 129 ff., 149 f., 156, 165, 169, 172, 191.
United Secession Church, 129 f.
Unity, 31, 38, 92, 95, 118, 170, 187, 193 f.

Veto Act, 134 f., 136 f., 141 155.
Voluntaryism, 125 f., 127 ff., 149.

Welsh, John, 78 f.
Westminster Assembly, 71, 186.
Westminster Confession, 52, 71, 72, 75, 94, 97, 99, 129, 132, 149, 150, 164, 169, 171, 191.
Whyte, Dr Alexander, 147.
Wilkie, William, 113.
William, King, the Lion, 34 f.
William, King, III., 83, 93 ff.
Willock, John, 48, 51.
Wilson, Margaret, 81.
Wilson, William, 105, 111.
Wishart, Bishop Robert, 36.
Wishart, George, 43 f., 46.
Woman's Guild, 4, 168, 181.
Worship, Family, 53, 89, 99, 147.
Worship, Public, 26, 50, 53, 61, 65 f., 69, 70 ff., 86, 96, 97, 146, 158 f., 165, 180, 186, 187.

PRINTED BY GILMOUR & DEAN LTD. GLASGOW AND LONDON